BOTTLE BIOLOGY

An idea book
for exploring the
world through
plastic bottles
and other
recyclable
materials

 KENDALL/HUNT PUBLISHING COMPANY
2460 Kerper Boulevard P.O. Box 539 Dubuque, Iowa 52004-0539

i

Writer	Mrill Ingram
Design	Lori Graham Mrill Ingram
Illustrator	Amy Kelley
Bottle Biology	Paul Williams John Greenler Robin Greenler Lori Graham Mrill Ingram Lisa Kehle David Eagan

Bottle Biology would like to extend special thanks to Judith Fischer, Jim Leidel, Lucy Slinger, Jane Scharer, Coe Williams, and the teachers and staff of the AgriScience Institute for their creativity, insight and support.

Bottle Biology, an instructional materials development program, was funded by a grant from the National Science Foundation administered by the University of Wisconsin-Madison.

Teachers may copy selected pages for student use.

CONTENTS

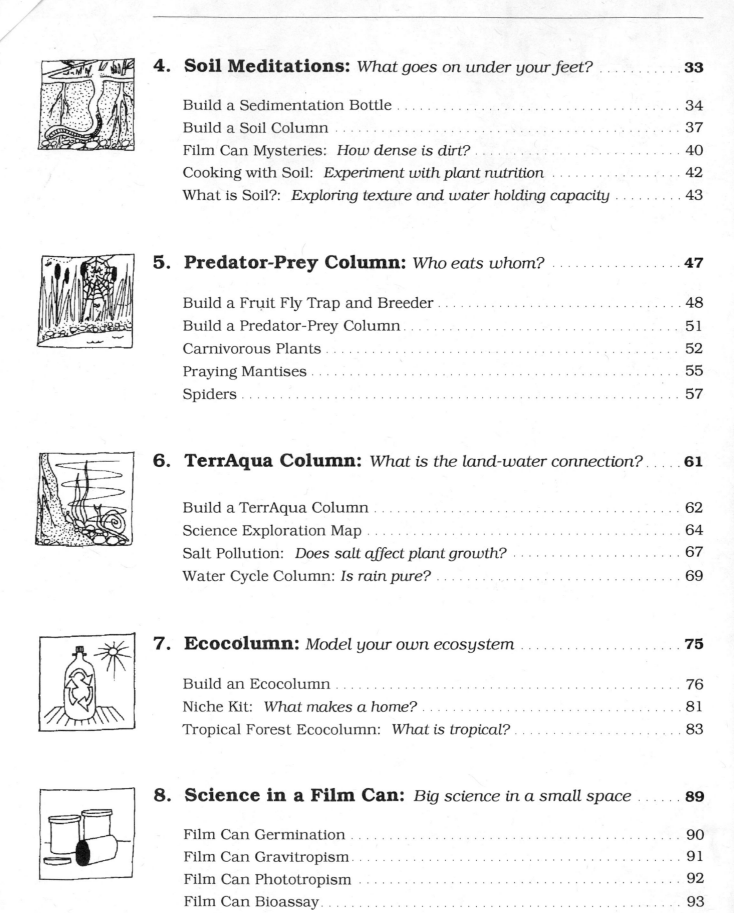

Discover the world in a bottle

INTRODUCTION

Hands-on, eyes-on, noses-on, mouths-on, minds-on: If you combine science with a soda bottle, what do you get? Two liters of soda pop orbiting Earth might be one result. But did you know you can use bottles to create an ecosystem, explore the concept of niche, and model a lake shore? You may have made a tornado in a bottle, but have you used bottles to breed fruit flies and spiders, to observe the adventures of slime molds or to pickle your own cabbage? Have you made a bottle microscope, a bottle timer or bottle tweezers?

Bottle Biology is an "idea book," full of ways you can use recyclable containers to learn about science and the environment. The projects in this book promote science as a tool everyone can use to explore the world. These explorations can be integrated with history, art, music and other creative endeavors.

Out of the trash, into the classroom: You'll find the materials you need for Bottle Biology in your trash can, backyard, supermarket, neighborhood park and recycling center. Bottle Biology uses materials that are local and inexpensive, exploding the myth that science belongs only to people with Ph.D.s, white coats and labs full of expensive glassware.

Like many good things in life, the inspiration for Bottle Biology arose unexpectedly — in this case from a pile of autumn leaves. While raking his garden one day, Paul Williams, a professor of Plant Pathology at the University of Wisconsin-Madison, asked himself what might be going on in the middle of the large compost pile he was creating. Why not put some of the leaves in an empty soda bottle and watch them to find out, he wondered. The result: The Decomposition Column and the beginning of Bottle Biology.

PLASTIC ONLY

RECYCLING

Leaves were the first things to go into bottles, followed closely by cabbage, soil, growing plants, praying mantises, and much more. After three years of Bottle Biology development, funded by the National Science Foundation, we put what we learned into this book. We hope it is an inspiration to integrate science into your teaching, or imagination into your science.

Bottle Biology Tips

Make your own bottle constructions before introducing them to others: Cutting bottles is easy but a little practice can vastly improve your technique. By making constructions before you introduce them to a classroom or a workshop, you can work out the details and any unexpected hitches. You will also provide your audience with a model to aspire to, or even surpass.

Do Bottle Biology in cooperative groups: The mechanics of cutting bottles, the planning and filling of columns, and the observation and exploration of each project are ideal jobs for two or three students working together. Group projects can foster student discussion and also cut down on the number of columns taking up precious space.

Allow plenty of time for group discussion: The Bottle Biology projects in this book have been developed to provoke discussion on a wide range of topics. We provide ideas with each chapter. Before diving into a construction, lead a class discussion about issues raised by the project, and what in particular you and your students would like to explore.

Reserve your right not to answer a good question: You can use Bottle Biology to promote the idea that science is not a lengthy list of facts, but a tool for exploration. When students ask questions, encourage them to think about the information they have, to predict possible answers, and to form their own methods of inquiry. See the Science Exploration Chart for an illustration of this idea (p. 64).

Improvise with Bottle Biology: This book is not the final word. Bottle Biology should be adapted to fit specific needs and interests. The techniques in this book will need to be modified as the world of plastic containers continues to evolve. Also, don't worry about repeating Bottle Biology activities. Every time you do an activity, you'll discover something new.

Adapt Bottle Biology for any skill level: Bottle Biology is currently used in classrooms from kindergarten to college. Most of the activities can be adapted to teach a wide variety of subjects at different levels.

The chapters towards the back of this book, such as the TerrAqua Column, the Ecocolumn and Science in a Film Can, include slightly more involved constructions and emphasize forming hypotheses and experimental design.

Constructions toward the front of the book, such as the Decomposition Column and Kimchee focus on observation and exploration and are easier to construct. If you foresee problems with students handling scissors, you can pre-cut bottle parts, perhaps with the assistance of a helpful parent. Students can then assemble and explore, but don't need to cut.

Bottle Biology is for teachers, parents and all students. Anyone can use soda bottles and other items from unexpected places to nurture new ideas and explore exciting science, in and out of the classroom.

What you will find in a chapter

 **CONNECTIONS** The introduction to each chapter describes a bottle activity along with associated issues and concepts. The "Connections" icon occurs on the first page of every chapter to indicate discussion topics and scientific process skills.

 BUILD "Build" pages show you how to assemble each column, and can be copied and distributed as worksheets.

 FILL Following the "Build" sections, you will find a "Fill" icon suggesting what to put in each column and where to find it.

 **OBSERVE** "Observe" sections indicate what to watch, smell, feel, and listen for after you've filled your column.

 **EXPLORE** Below the "Explore" icons you'll find activities and experiments for each column.

 *Background Reading* These sections provide background information to help you answer questions about your activities, or at least to give you novel conversation topics.

 **EXTENSION** The "Extension" icon indicates a supplemental activity involving a new construction, which allows you to further explore ideas in a chapter.

 *Additional Reading* If you don't find the answers you need in the Background Reading sections, look for references here.

More information: The following list of books and articles includes curriculum materials for hands-on science activities as well as general discussions about teaching science.

Blueford, Joyce 1989. "A Guide to Hands-on Science." *Science and Children*, 26(4): 20-21. *A guide to setting up your elementary classroom for hands-on science exploration.*

Cohen, Joy & Eve Pranis 1990. *GrowLab Activities for Growing Minds.* Burlington, VT: National Gardening Association. *A hands-on science curricula that uses plants to bring science and students to life, K-8.*

Driver, Rosalind 1985. *The Pupil as Scientist?* Philadelphia: The Open University Press. *This book investigates the difficulties and necessity of teaching scientific theory so that even very young students can be architects of their own knowledge.*

Graika, Tom 1989. "Minds-on, Hands-on Science." *Science Scope*, 12(6): 18-20. *Middle-school level procedures for turning on the creative and critical thinking skills.*

Hershey, David 1991. "Education: Linking History and Hands-on Biology." *BioScience*, 41(9): 628-630.

Medve, Richard & Frank Pugliese 1987. "Science as a Process: An Essential Component of the University Liberal Arts Philosophy." *The American Biology Teacher*, 49(5): 277-281.

Microcosmos: The Microcosmos Curriculum Guide to Exploring Microbial Space 1992. Dubuque, IA: Kendall/Hunt. *Aimed at 7th-9th grades, this teacher-developed collection of activities will teach microbe appreciation to students at any level.*

Science and Technology for Children 1992. "Experiments with Plants," and "Ecosystems." A project of the National Science Resource Center (NSRC). Burlington, NC: Carolina Biological Supply Company. *The NSRC has developed a number of excellent curriculum materials for hands-on science activities, all levels.*

Stencel, John 1990. "Community Biology: Getting Students Involved in Studying the Biology of Their Community." *The American Biology Teacher*, 52(2): 102-103.

Sumrall, William & Fred Brown 1991. "Consumer Chemistry in the Classroom: Science from the Supermarket." *The Science Teacher*, 58(4): 28-31.

Williams, Paul 1991. *Exploring with Fast Plants*. Madison: University of Wisconsin Press. *Elementary/middle school level exploratory approach in plant biology with rapid cycling brassicas, Wisconsin Fast Plants.*

Wrhen, Linda & Michael DiSpezio 1991. "Solid Waste Science: Rethink, Rework, Recycle." *Science and Children*, 28(7): 33. *An excellent elementary-level look at urban solid waste management.*

Chapter 1

Collecting, cleaning and cutting
BOTTLE BASICS

With a pair of scissors and your imagination, you can turn plastic soda bottles into tools for exploring the world. In this chapter we offer tips on how to collect, clean, cut and join bottles.

Anatomy: The first step in any construction project is to understand your materials. Take a look at the accompanying diagram. Note how the bottle tapers at the shoulder and hip. Because of this shape, you can "nest" the tapered ends inside the straight sides of another bottle.

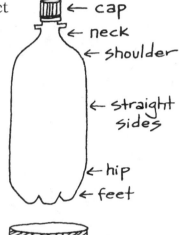

Species: Not all bottles are the same. Some have thinner, gently tapering bodies, while others are wider with rounder shoulders. Some bottles have separable bases, others stand on molded feet.

These differences will affect how your bottle constructions fit together. When you are collecting bottles to construct the columns in this book, look for bottles with similar shapes. One way to guarantee this is to use bottles of the same brand of beverage.

Footed bottles: Footed bottles and bottles with colored bases work equally well in Bottle Biology constructions. If a construction calls for a separate bottle base, you can substitute a footed base, cottage cheese dish, or other similarly shaped plastic container.

Bottle care: Creased and bent bottles have weak spots. Use bottles without dents so your columns are strong and durable. Also, remember that air expands and contracts with temperature changes. If you carry sealed bottles from a warm room to a cold car your bottles will crumple. When transporting bottles, keep the caps off or loosely attached to allow air exchange.

Nesting bottles

BOTTLE BIOLOGY TOOL KIT

These tools will enable you to construct any of the columns in this book. Some of these items are not critical – you do not need to use a razor to start bottle cuts, for example, or a tapered reamer to enlarge holes – but they can make construction easier.

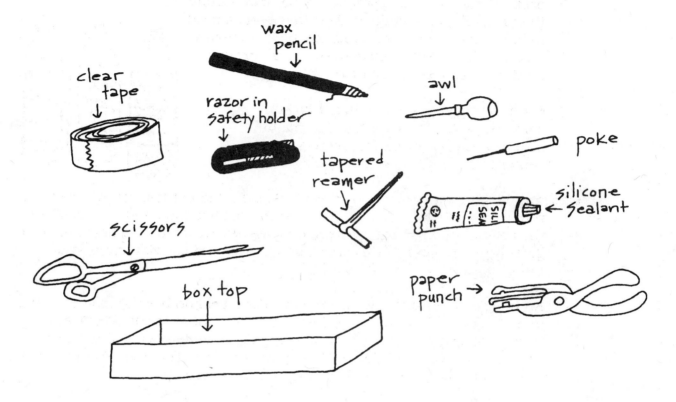

- **Box top or drawer** to stabilize bottle while making cutting lines;
- **Wax pencil, marker, or crayon** for drawing cutting lines;
- **Razor in safety holder or sharp pocket knife** to start cut;
- **Scissors** to cut bottle;
- **"Poke," darning needle or diaper pin** to make air holes;
- **Awl** to make holes in bottle caps and film cans;
- **Tapered reamer** for enlarging holes;
- **Paper punch** for making large holes in thin plastic;
- **Clear waterproof postal or bookbinding tape** to join columns;
- **Silicone sealant** to waterproof joints.

Collecting bottles: For better or for worse, plastic soda bottles are not difficult to come by. If your plans involve many bottles, however, you may need to organize some type of bottle collection activity. Some collection methods include:

- Becoming a very heavy soda drinker to create your own supply.

- Asking students to bring in bottles and/or establishing bottle drop-off points around your school or community. At the drop-off points make it clear that bottles need to be in good condition. Some teachers use extra credit points or other incentives to encourage students to contribute bottles.

- Collecting your own bottles from your community recycling center. You might also be able to arrange for the recycling center to set bottles aside for you.

Removing labels and bases: Once you have collected bottles, you will need to remove the labels and, depending on the construction and type of bottle, the colored bases. Most labels and bases are attached by a heat-sensitive glue. *Resist ripping off the labels, or you may end up with many small pieces of label stuck to the bottle.*

An inexpensive **hairdryer** will remove the label and base from your bottle in a jiffy. Set the hairdryer on **low**. Hold your bottle about 10 cm away from a blowing nozzle, and move it rapidly up and down so that the air warms the seam of the label. Gently pull on an edge of the label until you feel the glue begin to give. *This takes about 4 seconds.*

make hole in side just big enough for nozzle

blow dryer

move bottle fast so it doesn't melt!

5-gallon bucket

Bottles are made from PETE (polyethylene teraphthalate). This is a generally inert plastic, but it will warp easily if over-heated, so keep the bottle moving. (Leave the bottle cap on or fill the bottle with water first to prevent warping.)

To remove the base, heat the bottom of the base for about 15 seconds or until you can twist the colored base off the bottle.

A quieter way to remove the label and base from your bottle is to fill it about 1/4 full with **very warm water** *(49 - 65 degrees C or 120 - 150 degrees F; hotter than this may warp your bottle).* Cap the bottle in order to retain pressure inside so the bottle doesn't crumple, and tip it on its side to warm the glued seam. After a few seconds tug on a label corner.

Fill bottle 1/4 full with very warm water

keep cap on

tilt bottle to warm label

Once the label is off, stand the bottle on its end to soften the glue on the base, which can soon be twisted off. You may need to add new hot water. Some teachers have crockpots or coffee pots to ensure an adequate hot water supply.

Glue is often left on the bottle after the label is removed. If this offends your aesthetic sensibilities, rub a small amount of peanut butter onto the glue. As you rub, the oil in the peanut butter causes the glue to ball up so it can be pulled off (no kidding, crunchy works best). If you are really into the clean bottle look, wash your bottles with soap and water and dry them – they'll shine!

Cutting bottles: The easiest way to cut a bottle is to cut along a marked line with scissors. Once you have decided where to cut a bottle, place it on its side in the corner of an empty drawer, tray, or box — shallow cardboard flats and computer paper boxtops work well. Brace the bottom of the bottle against a corner of the box. Rest a pen or wax pencil against the edge of the box, so the tip rests against the bottle where you want your cutting line. Slowly turn the bottle. Two people make this job easy.

We use **wax (china) pencils** to make cutting lines because they don't smear and can be easily removed. Make sure your bottle is dry before marking. If you want lines that last, use a permanent marker.

Draw all of your cutting lines first (it's hard to do once the bottles have been cut), and then use a safety razor or utility knife to begin the bottle cuts. You only need a cut big enough to insert the top arm of a scissors. For some reason it is easier to cut a bottle with the top arm of the scissors inside the bottle, so insert the top arm into your initial cut and snip around, following your cutting line. Don't worry about ragged edges; they are easy to snip away with scissors once the bottle is in pieces.

On some constructions you may want to leave the base attached but expose more of the bottle for viewing. Cut away the sides of the base by sliding the bottom arm of a scissors between the base and bottle and cut a slit down toward the bottom. Then cut around the base to remove the sides.

insert scissors here

cut around base 1 cm from bottom

Making holes: The size, shape and number of air holes you put in a bottle column is part of your experiment – there's no wrong way to do it. Keep in mind, however, that with the Predator-Prey and the Decomposition Columns, you will most likely want holes small enough to keep fruit flies and other insects inside the bottle and out of your classroom. You will want adequate ventilation for plants, insects and other life, so make four or five "stars" of holes (see picture) – but keep them small.

You can make fancy designs with air holes

A **poke** is a needle, pin, or nail, with the blunt end stuck into a wooden handle. **Diaper pins, safety pins, upholstery needles** and **compass points** all work as well.

The instructions for making a small nail poke (see p. 6) also apply for needle and large nail pokes. For needle pokes, you needn't cut off the eye of the needle. For large nail poke handles, you may want to use a small dowel, and will need to drill a hole just a bit smaller than the nail into one end of the dowel in which to insert the cut end of the nail.

Hot pokes are useful for creating larger holes or making holes near the neck or base of the bottle where the plastic is thicker. Very large holes can be made by heating the open end of a glass test tube in a gas torch or Bunsen burner and pushing the tube through the bottle. Obviously, burns are a hazard of this technique.

Also, plastic smokes a bit as it melts, so an entire class using hot pokes can create a real stink. Be sure you let the pokes cool off in a safe place.

a candle works well for heating a needle or nail poke

Normally used for making small holes in leather and wood, the **woodworking awl** is quite effective at making small holes in bottles and caps. If an awl is pushed all the way through a surface, it will create a hole several millimeters wide, enough for fruit flies to pass through. Awls are particularly sharp, so place a piece of wood underneath whatever you are poking and watch your fingers. You can purchase awls at hardware stores.

poke hole in cap with awl...

...then enlarge with tapered reamer.

Also available at hardware stores, the **tapered reamer** is excellent for enlarging holes. Normally used for creating holes in sheet metal, it will easily make a hole in plastic up to 1 cm in diameter. Since the reamer has a blunt tip, begin your hole with an awl or poke.

A hand-held **paper punch** will easily penetrate a soda bottle or film can. Different punches create different sized and shaped holes. Since the holes are quite large, punches are not recommended for Predator-Prey Columns or Decomposition Columns.

If you are making many holes, invest in an inexpensive **motorized hand drill**. Regular spiral fluted drill bits work well, and sharp "brad" pointed bits will wander less on the surface of the plastic as you start your hole. For holes larger than 1 cm, flat wood bits with spurs on the blade tips work best. If you have access to one, a drill press is another efficient alternative.

How to Make a Small Nail Poke

branch piece

trim off

4-6 cm

1.5 cm

3-5 cm finishing nail

With wire cutters, cut off nail head at a sharp angle

press down HARD

hard wood surface

Poke head-end of nail into soft core (pith) of branch

Small nail poke

Pieces of old hosiery or no-see-um tent netting will keep out even the smallest flies. Use double-sided sticky tape to attach netting by surrounding the hole with tape and pressing on an appropriately sized piece of netting.

Pieces of old hosiery make good screens.

Joining bottles: Tape is the best material for joining bottles and will help columns survive handling in the classroom. However, not all tape is created equal.

Postal tapes that are clear, waterproof, and wide (about 5 cm), work well. For a large number of constructions, buy a dispenser. The best tape we have used (and the most expensive) is **bookbinding tape**. We use it for making demonstration constructions.

Some of the constructions you will make, particularly the Ecocolumn, require waterproof joints. Since even a waterproof tape will eventually leak, we recommend using a **silicone sealant**.

A few tricks when using silicone sealant:

• Silicone sets over a 24-hour period and is slippery when fresh. Fix the joint to be sealed with several small pieces of tape, which you can remove after the seal has solidified.

• Buy your sealant in a tube with a nozzle that you can fit as far into the joint as possible. This will give you a strong and watertight seal.

• Keep the silicone bead thin, 2-3 mm in diameter, so it sets in 24 hours.

• The chemicals used in silicone sealant are a health hazard. Use the stuff in a ventilated area.

Use silicone sealant in a WELL VENTILATED area!!

Film cans: Plastic 35 mm film cans come in very handy for many Bottle Biology projects. They make excellent water- and air-tight storage containers for seeds, soil, water samples and many important items. The Film Can Science chapter will show you how film cans provide the perfect containers for individual, portable experiments. There's nothing like a science experiment you can take home with you.

Both black and clear film cans are useful. You can obtain them free from places that process film. We have had good luck with film processors in local discount stores.

Scientific supply or lab supply companies: These companies are good sources of many different materials for classroom projects. For example, it's in the middle of January, and you are having trouble collecting insects and plants to fill your Ecocolumns. Through catalogs, these companies offer a wide variety of useful materials including plants, insects, lenses, fertilizers, kits for testing pH and soil, books and other teaching materials. We have listed a few companies here, but check your local Yellow Pages also.

- Carolina Biological Supply Company in Burlington, NC (800-334-5551) and Gladstone, OR (800-547-1733)
- Edmund Scientific Company in Barrington, NJ (609-573-6250)
- Connecticut Valley Biological in Southhampton, MA (800-628-7748)
- Science Kit & Boreal Labs in Tonawanda, NY (800-828-7777)
- Nasco Science in Fort Atkinson, WI (414-563-2446) and Modesto, CA (209-529-6957)

Wisconsin Fast Plants: In some of the plant experiments in this book, we mention Wisconsin Fast Plants. These small plants, related to cabbages and mustards, run through their entire life cycle, seed to seed, in just 35 days. Developed as a research tool, these plants are also appropriate for all sorts of classroom investigations. For more information write:

Wisconsin Fast Plants
1630 Linden Drive
University of Wisconsin-Madison
Madison, WI 53706

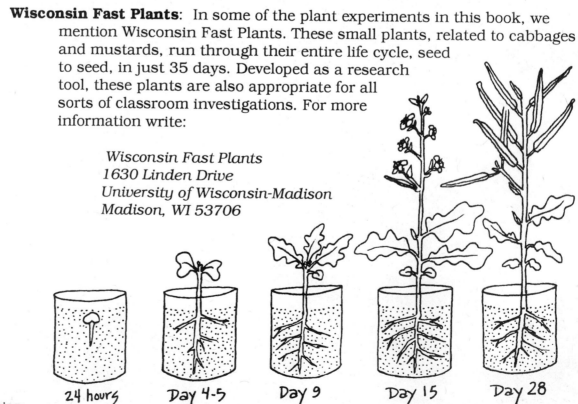

24 hours   Day 4-5   Day 9   Day 15   Day 28

Plastic 5-gallon buckets, postal scales, and other useful items: Large plastic buckets can be made into growbuckets for your plants (p. 105), or used to store many different items. They can often be obtained free from food service or manufacturing companies (check your school cafeteria).

Postal scales are excellent for weighing liquids and objects up to 3 ounces. They are available at stationery and postal supply stores. Other useful items include plastic straws, pipettes and microcentrifuge tubes, which can be used as water feeders and measuring devices. They can be obtained through lab supply companies.

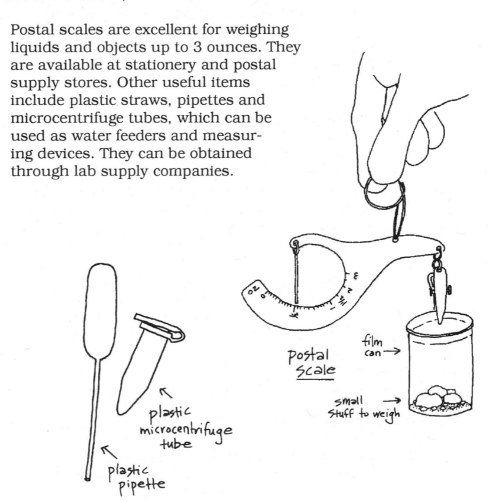

plastic microcentrifuge tube

plastic pipette

postal scale

film can →

small → stuff to weigh

Chapter 2

When is the end a beginning?

DECOMPOSITION COLUMN

The U.S. generates 190 million tons of solid waste a year — enough to fill a bumper-to-bumper convoy of garbage trucks halfway to the moon. So why aren't we up to our necks in garbage?

The key to staying on top of the garbage heap is recycling, by people and nature. People are just beginning to recycle some of the metal, glass and plastic that fill up a quarter of America's garbage pails.

Nature recycles garbage all the time, and this recycling is essential to the availability of nutrients for living things. Nature's recyclers are tiny bacteria and fungi, which break down plant and animal waste, making nutrients available for other living things in the process. This is known as decomposition.

Decomposition involves a whole community of large and small organisms that serve as food for each other, clean up each other's debris, control each other's populations and convert materials to forms that others can use. The bacteria and fungi that initiate the recycling process, for example, become food for other microbes, earthworms, snails, slugs, flies, beetles and mites, all of which in turn feed larger insects and birds.

You can think of the Decomposition Column as a miniature compost pile or landfill, or as leaf litter on a forest floor. Through the sides of the bottle you can observe different substances decompose and explore how moisture, air, temperature and light affect the process.

Many landfills seal garbage in the earth, excluding air and moisture. How might this affect decomposition? Will a foam cup *ever* rot? What happens to a fruit pie, or tea bag? Which do you think decomposes faster, banana peels or leaves? If you add layers of soil to the column, how might they affect the decomposition process? What would you like to watch decompose?

 **CONNECTIONS:** *microbial ecology, decomposition, food chains, carbon and nitrogen cycles, recycling, landfills. Scientific process skills — observing, predicting, asking questions, recording data, describing.*

BUILD:

DECOMPOSITION COLUMN

MATERIALS:

- three 2-liter soda bottles
- Bottle Biology Tool Kit (p. 2)
- kitchen scraps, leaves, newspapers ... you decide!

1. Remove labels from all 3 bottles. Remove bases from 2 of them if they have bases (see Bottle Basics, p. 3).

BOTTLE #1

2. Cut top off Bottle #1 2 to 3 cm below shoulder so that cylinder has straight sides.

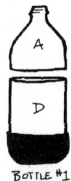

BOTTLE #1

3. Cut top off Bottle #2 2 to 3 cm above shoulder. Cut bottom off 2 to 3 cm below hip. The resulting cylinder will have two tapered ends.

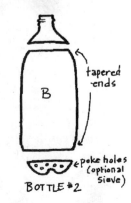

tapered ends

poke holes (optional sieve)

BOTTLE #2

4. Cut bottom off Bottle #3, 2 to 3 cm above hip, so cylinder has a straight end.

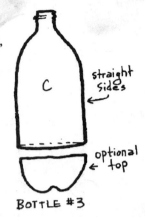

straight sides

optional top

BOTTLE #3

5. Invert "C" and stack into base "D". Stack "B" and tape middle seam securely. Poke air holes. Add top "A" with a piece of tape for a hinge.

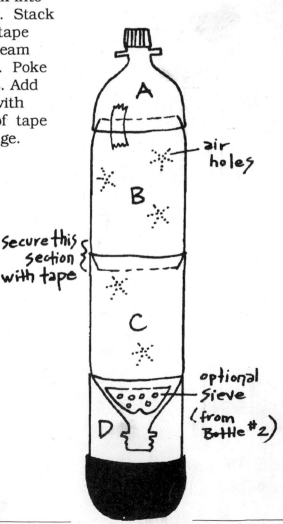

air holes

secure this section with tape

optional sieve (from Bottle #2)

FILL

Choosing ingredients: Decomposition Column ingredients can include leaves, grass and plant clippings, kitchen scraps, newspapers, animal manure and soil. If you are interested in how fast things decay, try building two identical columns, but fill them with leaves from two different species of trees. Try adding fertilizer to your column, or water from a pond or river. How do you suppose differences in temperature, light or moisture will affect the decomposition process?

The time it takes: You'll begin to see mold and other evidence of decomposition within the first few days after filling your column.

Two or three months is plenty of time to see soft **organic** material such as leaves, fruits, vegetables and grain products decompose dramatically. (The term organic applies to something that is derived directly from a living organism.) Bark, newspapers and wood chips all take longer to decompose, though they still undergo interesting changes in two to three months.

How wet?: Keep your column moist in order to observe more rapid decomposition. Avoid flooding your column or it will become waterlogged. This can create an **anaerobic** environment, or one completely lacking oxygen, in which certain microbes create particularly vigorous odors.

Using your nose: Odor is a by-product of decomposition, and can tell you a lot about the materials in your columns. Odors may be strong at first, but can mellow and become musty with time. Classrooms full of odorous Decomposition Columns, however, have been known to try the patience of colleagues and building supervisors. The strongest odors arise from animal products such as meat and dairy products. Grapefruit rinds and grass cuttings can also produce strong odors. Why is this so? If you use food scraps, mix in plant matter such as leaves, twigs and dried grass to temper odors. Layering soil on top of contents also lessens the odor.

Increasing the number and size of air holes in your column will increase air exchange. How do you think this will affect decomposition? Keep holes small so fruit flies stay inside.

If your classroom fruit fly population booms anyway, make a Fruit Fly Trap! (p. 48). See Bottle Basics (p.5), for more information on making holes.

AIR HOLES

Recording data: Once you've decided how to fill your column, carefully observe what you put inside. In a notebook, describe the color, texture, smell and shape of everything you put in the bottle. Weigh everything before it goes into the column, (see the Bottle Balance, p. 115).

Schedule column checks for at least once a week to record changes. Note changes in the column contents' height, color, shape, texture and odor. Hold a ruler next to the column to record changes in the height of the contents. Insert a thermometer from the top of the column to determine temperature changes. Can you figure out the rate of change? You can also test the pH of the leachate (the solution that drips through the column) or use it in a bioassay (p. 93). See p. 26 for more on pH.

Is anything moving?: Look for the appearance of any "critters," such as flies, beetles, slugs, millipedes, or snails. Decomposition Columns offer good opportunities for observation and description. Try using photographs or drawings to record changes. Write a story about what is going on in your column. What do you predict will happen during decomposition?

"On Top"

All this new stuff goes on top
turn it over turn it over
wait and water down.
From the dark bottom
turn it inside out
let it spread through, sift down,
even.
Watch it sprout.

A mind like compost.

Gary Snyder, 1983   *Axe Handles*

Rot Race: A decomposition experiment

Soil or no soil?: Build two Decomposition Columns. Weigh out equal quantities of leaves from the same tree. Fill both columns loosely, but mix about 125 ccs (half a cup) of garden soil in one. (You can also experiment with grass or other plant material.)

Pour equal amounts of pond or rainwater (200 to 400 mls or 1 to 2 cups) into each column and wait several hours for the water to soak through. Add enough, in equal amounts, so that about 125 mls (half a cup) drips into the bottom reservoir. Schedule one of these "rainstorms" to occur in the column every few days, pouring the drained water back through the column. Which leaf column decomposes faster, and why?

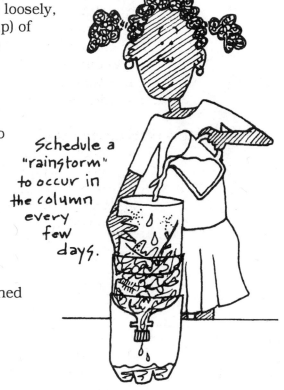

Schedule a "rainstorm" to occur in the column every few days.

Jim Leidel's 6th-grade students in Madison, WI build Decomposition Columns and try to model natural systems. Some students, for example, pour vinegar solutions through their columns in order to model acid rainfall. Vinegar solutions are also poured through limestone and granitic gravel buffers in order to imitate what might be occurring in eastern U.S. lakes. Levels of pH are measured and compared.

In the past, Jim's students tested solutions of their own choosing, among which were tomato juice and sugar water.

What Is All That Rot?

A bit on the microbiology of decomposition

Decomposition can be thought of as a parade of many very tiny creatures. How decomposition proceeds in your column depends on which bacteria and fungi inhabit it, what ingredients you have put inside, and environmental factors such as light, temperature and moisture.

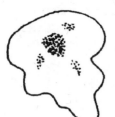

amoeba

The first decomposing organisms that go to work attack the most available food molecules, such as sugars, carbohydrates and proteins. As they grow, these first bacteria and fungi also change the environment. For example, they produce heat, change the pH and consume oxygen. You will see these changes in your column as plant parts become dark and slimy.

As they change their own environment, these organisms can create conditions that favor competing microbes. The biological definition of **succession** is the replacement of one type of organism by another,

fungi

often caused by environmental changes wrought by the first organism.

In your Decomposition Column, for example, one type of bacteria might flourish, changing the pH and raising the temperature of the column in the process. These new conditions may be favorable for a more heat tolerant type of bacteria, which will take over the original bacteria.

A Decomposition Column will show you the dynamic process of decay: strange white fuzz may appear and cover your column for a few days before suddenly disappearing to be replaced by a dark fuzz that climbs up one side. You might see something orange and slimy moving slowly along a rotting twig. You may also observe non-microbial life such as fruit flies, mites and millipedes.

bacteria

Bacteria, fungi, algae, protozoa and other organisms that live on dead or decaying matter are collectively known as **saprophytes**.

Saprophytes often secrete enzymes onto material they want to eat. Enzymes are biochemicals, responsible for all kinds of chemical reactions including the breakdown of matter into digestible parts for the decomposers. A crumbling log lying on the forest floor, for example, shows the work of enzymes made by saprophytes.

Bacteria are the most numerous of the decomposers. Good soil may have 100 to 1,000 million bacteria per gram. You may see bacterial colonies as round spots, ranging from white, to cream, to brown in color.

There are many types of bacteria. You might identify one type by its odor. These bacteria, called **actinomycetes**, live in the soil and are responsible for that fresh, earthy smell that accompanies newly plowed soil, or a long awaited summer rain.

Fungi might appear in your column as a fuzzy blanket of mold covering some delectable rotting thing. Mold fungi form mazes of tiny threads called **mycelium**. If you look closely you may see tiny dots along the threads. These dots are fruiting bodies, which release fungal spores. A particularly common mold, *Rhizopus*, has a cottony appearance with black dots, and often shows up on bread, fruits and other food.

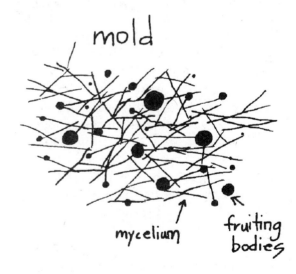

mold

mycelium

fruiting bodies

Slime molds are organisms that move, feeding on microorganisms such as bacteria. They are often brightly colored and have the appearance and consistency of pudding. Slime molds often move toward light, leaving snail-like tracks behind, and producing numerous tiny fruiting bodies, some resembling tiny mushrooms.

Algae might show up in your column as a green tinge on the soil surface or on a moist twig. You have probably seen algae, like **Spirogyra**, growing on the banks of a river, a lake, or perhaps the sides of a fish tank, or as seaweed in the ocean.

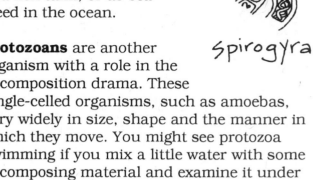

Spirogyra

Protozoans are another organism with a role in the decomposition drama. These single-celled organisms, such as amoebas, vary widely in size, shape and the manner in which they move. You might see protozoa swimming if you mix a little water with some decomposing material and examine it under a microscope.

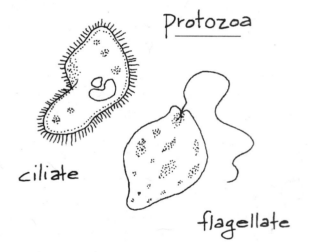

Protozoa

ciliate

flagellate

Although much of the action takes place on a microscopic scale, decomposition is an exciting process even to the naked eye. By studying your Decomposition Column you can get a sense of the great diversity and activity of microbial life. Bacteria, fungi, algae and protozoa may be small but they are responsible for a great deal of change.

note: Some of these organisms can only be seen with a microscope

Worm Composting:

Never underestimate the power of a worm

Worms play a major role in breaking down plant matter and creating fertile soil. Earthworms eat fallen leaves and other plant parts. Their droppings, or "castings," fertilize the soil. As they tunnel into the earth, they move leaves and other organic matter downward, and bring deeper soil to the surface. This tunneling and mixing aerates the soil so that plant roots and water penetrate more easily. Observe wonderful worm activity for yourself by building a worm column.

Some species of earthworms live in leaf litter. Others dwell several meters below the soil surface.

The best worms to use in your column are **red worms**. Red worms consume lots of organic material, survive well in captivity and reproduce quickly.

Red worms are **not** the same worms you find in your garden soil, though you might find them in garden, leaf and compost piles, or manure piles around stables and barns.

Red worms can be bought at bait shops. If no one fishes where you live, or you need worms in the dead of winter, try ordering them from a lab supply company (p. 8).

We have had good luck with a company dedicated to home vermicomposting: Flowerfield Enterprises in Kalamazoo, MI, (616) 327-0108. They sell red worms by the pound, which is about 200 red worms.

BUILD:

WORM COLUMN

MATERIALS:

- Bottle Biology Tool Kit (see p. 2)
- one 2-liter bottle
- one bottle base from another bottle or a similarly shaped container for a top
- one large brown paper bag, or one 25 cm x 40 cm sheet of brown paper for a screen
- 15 - 20 red worms per column
- worm bedding: shredded newspaper, shredded leaves, peat moss and straw all work well.
- worm food: organic leftovers from your kitchen, garden or yard, especially plant material

1. Remove the label from your soda bottle and cut the top off about 10 cm below the top.

If your bottle has a base, cut the sides off. Use a second base, or another small plastic container for the column top.

cut off 10 cm from top

trim base for better viewing

2. Poke four 5 mm drainage holes with a large hot nail poke low around the base. Poke two rows of eight 3 mm airholes with a small hot poke. (See p. 5 for poke instructions.)

air holes

drainage

3. Cut the brown paper so it encircles the column and extends about 4 cm higher. Tape the paper around the column but leave it loose so you can easily pull it up. Worms prefer the dark, so leave the screen on the bottle unless you are observing the worms and their work.

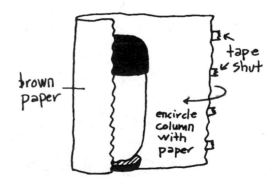

tape shut

brown paper

encircle column with paper

FILL

Bedding

Making newspaper bedding: To make enough bedding for four columns, cut 8 to 10 pages of newsprint into strips 0.5 cm wide, then cut these strips in half crosswise.

Worms breathe through their skin so they need a moist environment. Add 400 to 600 mls of water (2-3 cups) to the bedding, and then fluff it vigorously until the paper strips are well separated. Add a small handful of soil into the bedding to introduce natural soil microorganisms, which help break down the paper.

Fill the worm column two-thirds full with the bedding. Worms prefer a neutral or slightly basic environment (a pH of 6.5-8.5), so mix in some powdered lawn lime or finely crushed eggshells if a pH test indicates acidic bedding (see p. 26). Whatever type of bedding you use, make sure it is quite moist, but not saturated with water. Place 15-20 worms on top of the bedding. They will find their own way into the bedding.

What temperature?: The temperature of your column should stay within 20 to 25 degrees C (68 to 77 degrees F).

Feeding your worms: Worms can't live off of newsprint alone! You will need to add organic food every 3 to 4 days — any sort of plant material works well such as kitchen waste and leaves. Worms feed by sucking or pumping material into their bodies with a muscular pharynx, so the food should be moist and in small (1-2 cm) pieces. Place food on the bedding and cover it with about 1-2 cm of moist bedding. Check to see if the food is being eaten before adding more. A rule of thumb: Worms need 2 or 3 times their mass of food every few days. *(This is approximately 70 to 100 grams of food for 15 to 20 red worms.)* If in doubt, it's better to slightly underfeed them.

WORM CONDOMINIUM

*Although worms survive well in bottles, **five gallon buckets** and other larger containers make it easier to maintain larger worm colonies for longer periods of time.*

A hand drill will help you make drainage and aeration holes in buckets. Make the holes about 1 cm in diameter. Fill the bucket only a little over half full with bedding. Keep the lid on the bucket at all times to keep light out and moisture in.

Additional Reading

Anderson, Lucia 1987. "Does Microbiology Belong in Elementary Schools?" *Science and Children*, 25(1): 26-28. *This author thinks so — and offers her ideas on how to make it happen.*

Campbell, S. 1989 *Let it Rot: The Home Gardener's Guide to Composting.* Pownal, VT: Garden Way Publishing, Storey Communications. *A down-to-earth gardening book, with a lay person's account of compost science.*

Cobb, Vicki 1981. *Lots of Rot.* New York: J. B. Lippincott. *An entertaining elementary-level introduction to the business of decomposition and the amazing creatures that carry it out.*

Golueke, C. G. 1972. *Composting: A Study of the Process and its Principles.* Emmaus, PA: Rodale Press. *An upper-level text on the science of composting.*

Jones, Linda 1992. "Strike it Rich with Classroom Compost." *The American Biology Teacher*, 54(7):420-424. *A well-designed high school-level activity with an observation chart.*

Rodale, J. I. et. al. 1975. *The Complete Book of Composting.* Emmaus, PA: Rodale Books, Inc.

Yanagita, Tomomichi 1990. *Natural Microbial Communities: Ecological and Physiological Features.* Tokyo: Japan Scientific Societies Press. *A well-written, graduate-level text on microbes in the soil, water and atmosphere.*

Reading on worms

Appelhof, Mary 1982. *Worms Eat My Garbage.* Michigan: Flower Press. *An excellent, accessible guide to setting up and maintaining a worm composting system.*

Kourik, Robert 1992. "As the Worm Turns." *Garbage Magazine.* Jan/Feb 4: 48. *An article on Mary Appelhof, author of* Worms Eat My Garbage.

McGuire, Daniel 1987. "Project Worm Bin." *Science and Children*, 24(6): 11-12.

McLaughlin, M. 1986. *Earthworms, Dirt, and Rotten Leaves, An Exploration in Ecology.* New York: Atheneum. *A friendly, informative exploration of earthworm biology and ecology, including several activities for all ages.*

Does fermentation lead to good taste?

KIMCHEE

What pickles a cuke? Is yogurt alive? Where does Swiss cheese get its holes? How is pizza dough made?

These questions all relate to **fermentation,** a process people use to create and preserve many types of food.

The term "fermentation" refers to the activity of bacteria and fungi, such as yeast (which is a single-celled fungus). These microbes break complex compounds, like sugars, into simpler substances, such as carbon dioxide and alcohol. Because these simpler substances are toxic to food-spoiling microbes, they act as natural preservatives for food.

Before refrigeration, fermentation was a primary method of food preservation. Builders working on China's 1,500-mile-long Great Wall in the early part of this millennium ate cabbage fermented in wine.

Genghis Khan's forces carried pickled food with them on their invasions of eastern Europe in the 12th century. In the early 18th century, the British Navy carried pickled cabbage to provide sailors with vitamin C in order to prevent scurvy.

Kimchee is a traditional fermented cabbage dish from Korea. Koreans eat kimchee year round for the spicy taste and because it contains lots of vitamins C and B.

You may be more familiar with the traditional German pickled cabbage dish, **sauerkraut**, a less spicy version of kimchee.

In a bottle fermentation chamber you can pickle your own cabbage. You'll learn a lot about fermentation, and enjoy great-tasting results.

KIMCHEE
Date — pH —
Date — pH —

CONNECTIONS: *cultural food traditions, food preservation, anaerobic fermentation, microbial ecology (Lactobacillus), pH, math, chemistry. Scientific process skills — observing, recording data, using the senses, making measurements, graphing.*

BUILD:

FERMENTATION CHAMBER

MATERIALS:
- one 2-liter soda bottle
- one plastic lid about 9 cm across
- one 2-3 lb. head of Chinese cabbage (*Brassica rapa*), also called napa or petsai, cut into 4 cm chunks. (For sauerkraut use European round-headed green cabbage.)
- chopped hot chili pepper, or chili powder
- two cloves garlic, thinly sliced
- 20 grams (3 tsp) non-iodized (pickling or kosher) salt
- pH paper or red cabbage juice (p. 26)
- Bottle Biology Tool Kit (p. 2)

1. Remove the label from a 2-liter soda bottle. (See p. 3.)

2. Cut the top off the bottle just 1 cm below shoulder.

leave very little of straight side

3. Layer cabbage, garlic, pepper, and a sprinkling of salt into the bottle. (If you are making sauerkraut use round green cabbage and omit garlic and chili.) Repeat layers until the bottle is packed full, placing the plastic lid on each layer and pressing down vigorously to break up the cabbage and distribute the salt.

LAYER:

salt

cabbage

chili

garlic

NOTE: Be careful to WASH YOUR HANDS after working with chili peppers (or it might get in your eyes!)

4. Press down occasionally over the next hour or two. You can also use a quart Mason jar or freezer bag filled with water, or a peanut butter jar.

Using a weight (like a peanut butter jar) can make pressing the cabbage easier.

5. After a few hours, the cabbage should fill 1/2 to 2/3 of the bottle. Slide the bottle top inside, forming a sliding seal. Push down so no air remains under the lid. The cabbage must be submerged at all times. You can also leave the jar or bag on top of the plastic lid.

When the pH drops to about 3.5 (3 days to 2 weeks), your kimchee or sauerkraut is ready!

The cabbage should be covered by a layer of juice at all times.

How pickling proceeds: Fermentation is the work of millions of microbes. You can't see them without a microscope, but you can **see, smell and taste** evidence of their activity.

Each day, press down on the jar or bottle top so that cabbage juice always covers the cabbage, and the cabbage is kept from contact with the air. You are cultivating **anaerobes**, organisms that grow best where there is no oxygen. As you press down on the cabbage, you will see bubbles of carbon dioxide (CO_2) rising to the surface. Where do they come from?

How long does it take?: Cabbage can take 3 days to 2 weeks to complete fermentation, depending on the surrounding temperature. The warmer it is, the faster it ferments. If your classroom is a steady 25 degrees C (75 degrees F) or more, you can have kimchee within 4 days sauerkraut requires more like two weeks.

Measure the **acidity** of the cabbage juice with pH paper daily (see p. 26). You can record the date and pH directly on the paper strips, and then tape them on the bottle to keep track of changes. (Try graphing the changes in pH. See graph p. 29.)

Pass the bottle around and get help pressing.

Your kimchee or sauerkraut is ready to eat when the pH of the cabbage juice has dropped from about pH 6.5 to pH 3.5. You'll have to open the sliding seal in order to taste the cabbage. When you remove the top, however, the bottle's contents are exposed to air, which may allow different kinds of microbes to grow. To be safe, refrigerate after opening. Do not eat the kimchee or sauerkraut if mold is present.

Smell and taste your kimchee: Do you notice the **aroma** of garlic and pepper? How do the odors change with time? Can you taste the garlic and the pepper? You can explore flavors by adding other ingredients such as ginger, radishes, or different amounts of pepper and garlic.

One bottle will give everyone in a class of 20 a taste

Acids and Bases: Make your own pH indicator

What is pH?: The terms **acid** and **base** describe chemical characteristics of many substances that we use daily. We use bases to make soaps and detergents, for example. Almost all the foods we eat, from bread to coffee, are slightly acidic.

The pH scale is a measure of acidity. You can buy pH indicator paper from any biological or lab supply company (p. 8), which can be used to give you an accurate measurement of the acidic or basic quality of substances you want to test. You can also make your own pH indicator using red cabbage juice, for example, to track the changing pH in your fermentation chamber.

Make your own acid/base indicator: Blend 2 cups chopped red cabbage leaves and 1 cup water in a food processor or electric blender until pieces are tiny and uniform. Strain the liquid. You can also chop the cabbage coarsely and boil it in the water for about 5 minutes until the

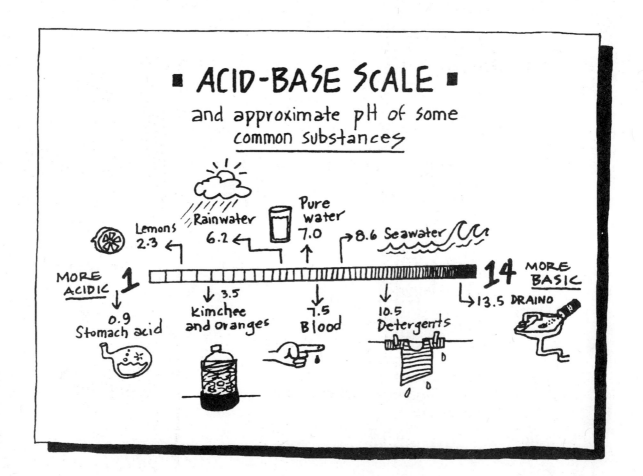

liquid is dark purple. This purple liquid will change color according to the acidity or alkalinity (basic quality) of substances you want to test.

Add about 10 drops of cabbage juice to approximately 1 tablespoon of a test substance. What color does cabbage juice turn in an acid like white vinegar? What about in a base such as a baking soda solution?

Test the pH of various substances and develop a corresponding color-pH scale. Compare your results with the chart here.

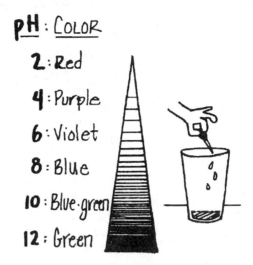

pH : COLOR
2 : Red
4 : Purple
6 : Violet
8 : Blue
10 : Blue-green
12 : Green

You can also make **indicator paper** by dipping strips of white paper towel, coffee filters, or construction paper into the cabbage juice until they are purple. When the purple strips are dry, use a toothpick, soda straw or eye dropper to place a drop of a test solution on the strips. How do the results compare to your pH chart?

What Does the Salt Do? Osmosis and density changes in Kimchee

Osmosis: When you sprinkle salt on cabbage leaves and then exert pressure on them, you'll notice that the leaves become limp and the bottle begins to fill with liquid. Just what is going on here?

Liquid inside the cells of the cabbage leaves is flowing out of the cells in response to the salt, a phenomenon called **osmosis**.

Osmosis is the movement of fluid through a membrane in order to create an equal concentration of dissolved solids (salt, in this case) in the fluid on either side of the membrane.

"OSMOSIS" is a balancing act

When you salt a cabbage leaf, you create a difference in salt concentration — higher outside the cabbage leaf and lower inside the cells. In order to equalize the salt concentration, water from inside the cabbage leaf cells will exit through the cell membranes. The water will continue to flow out of the cells until there is an equal concentration of salt in the fluids on either side of the cell wall, or until the cell is completely dehydrated.

1000 grams of water + 20 grams of salt = a 2% solution.

One 2-liter soda bottle of water = 1000 gm

½ film can = 20 gm salt

SALT

The 2% solution: People who pickle often use a 2% salt concentration. How much salt must you add to your 2-liter bottle of cabbage to produce a 2% salt concentration?

It just so happens that a 2-liter soda bottle packed full of cabbage leaves weighs approximately 1 kilogram. Chinese cabbage is about 95% water, so you need only to figure out how much salt you need to add to 1 kilogram (1,000 grams) of water in order to create a 2% solution. Two percent of 1,000 (.02 x 1,000) is 20 — you need 20 grams of salt. Since one 35 mm film can holds 40 grams of salt, a film can half full of salt is a good measure of what you will need.

Density changes: During the first few hours after you fill your kimchee bottle, you will observe that the height of cabbage leaves falls by half. The weight of the bottle remains the same, but the density changes. How can you quantify the density changes in your 2-liter bottle?

DENSITY

$$d = g/v$$

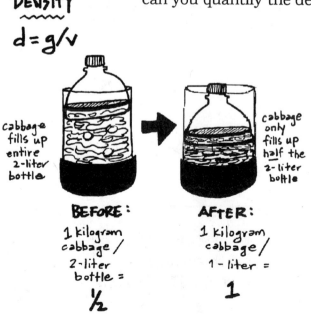

cabbage fills up entire 2-liter bottle

cabbage only fills up half the 2-liter bottle

BEFORE:
1 kilogram cabbage / 2-liter bottle =
½

AFTER:
1 kilogram cabbage / 1-liter =
1

A 2-liter bottle newly packed full of leaves weighs about a kilogram. Since density is grams per volume (d=g/v), your kimchee or sauerkraut has an initial density of 1 kilogram of cabbage per 2-liter soda bottle, or 1/2.

Due to osmosis, however, the cabbage level drops to about half the bottle. In other words, the volume drops to 1 liter. Now the density equals 1 kilogram per 1 liter, or 1. The mass of the bottle hasn't changed, but the density has doubled.

Good Bug, Bad Rap
An introduction to fermentation

Microbes get a pretty bad rap. We give them long, complicated names like *Streptococcus thermophilus*, or else we call them something negative like "germs." But we depend on microorganisms in every realm of life, from producing the food we eat to cycling energy in our ecosystems.

Meet **Lactobacillus.** This friendly microbe lives just about everywhere, including in dairy products and on fruits and vegetables. Most types of *Lactobacillus* wouldn't hurt a flea (though they might change your milk into yogurt). We use *Lactobacillus* to make yogurt, as well as cheese, buttermilk, soy sauce and kimchee.

Lactobacillus is an anaerobe, which means it grows best in environments lacking oxygen (though it has no trouble living with oxygen; it just slows down).

When you make kimchee, you set up a very friendly environment for *Lactobacillus* by filling a bottle with cabbage and adding salt, which helps to release water and sugars from the cabbage cells. By keeping the cabbage submerged in cabbage juice, you create an anaerobic environment.

This combination of no oxygen and lots of sugar is a paradise for *Lactobacillus*, which happens to be quite fond of sugar. It will happily eat up the

sugars and churn out lactic acid, a habit that gives the microbe its name.

This activity is at the heart of kimchee fermentation. The more sugar *Lactobacillus* eats, the more lactic acid it produces, and this is why the pH of your kimchee drops over time. *Lactobacillus* grows best at a pH of about 5. The accompanying chart shows how pH, glucose (or sugar), and lactic acid all change over time in kimchee fermentation.

There are several species of *Lactobacillus*, which fall into two major groups depending on what they produce after eating sugars. The *homofermentative* bacteria produce one thing: lactic acid.

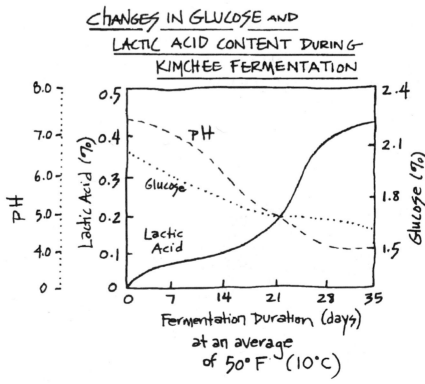

CHANGES IN GLUCOSE AND LACTIC ACID CONTENT DURING KIMCHEE FERMENTATION

Fermentation Duration (days) at an average of 50° F (10°C)

Heterofermenters produce lactic acid and other products, including ethanol and CO_2. Both types of *Lactobacillus* help the fermentation process in kimchee, specifically, the homofermentative bacteria *Lactobacillus plantarum* and the heterofermentative type *Lactobacillus brevis.*

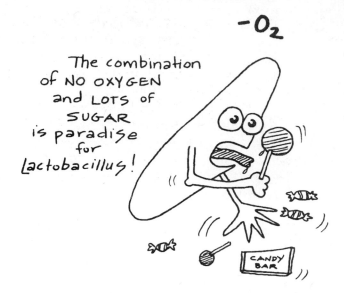

$-O_2$

The combination of NO OXYGEN and LOTS of SUGAR is paradise for *Lactobacillus*!

Additional Reading

Brock, Thomas & M. Madigan 1988. *Biology and Microorganisms* (5th Ed.). Menlo Park, CA: Benjamin/Cummins Publishing Co. *A well-written, college-level text on microbiology.*

Burns, Joe 1990 "The Cabbage Caper." *Science Scope,* 13(5): 28-31. *Middle school-level activities on acids and bases.*

Campbell-Platt, Geoffrey 1987. *Fermented Foods of the World: A Dictionary and Guide.* Boston: Butterworths. *A reference book that will take you on a culinary voyage.*

Chun, Jae Kun 1981. "Chinese Cabbage Utilization in Korea: Kimchi Processing Technology." *Chinese Cabbage,* N.S. Talekar & T.D. Griggs, eds. Taiwan China: Asian Vegetable Research and Development Center. *A technical discussion of the fermentation process in kimchee.*

Cobb, Vicki 1984. *More Science Experiments You Can Eat.* Philadelphia: J.B. Lippencott. *With lots of ideas for elementary and middle school levels, this book offers many entertaining ways to explore your kitchen laboratory, including making cheese and chocolate pudding.*

Levine, Elise 1990. "Fermentation is a Gas." *Science Scope,* 13(4): 22-24. *A middle school-level activity on yeast fermentation.*

McGee, Harold 1984. *On Food and Cooking.* New York: Scribner's. *A fascinating and comprehensive exploration of food and cooking, including food chemistry.*

Microcosmos: The Microcosmos Curriculum Guide to Exploring Microbial Space 1992. The Microcosmos Team. Dubuque, IA: Kendall/Hunt. *Aimed at 7th through 9th grades, this teacher-developed curriculum holds exciting teaching ideas for any level.*

Rupp, Rebecca 1987. *Blue Corn and Square Tomatoes.* Pownal, VT: Storey Communications, Inc. *An entertaining social history of a variety of vegetables.*

Sagan, Dorion & Lynn Margulis 1988. *Garden of Microbial Delights: A Practical Guide to the Subvisible World.* Boston: Harcourt Brace Jovanovich. *Difficult to find but well worth the effort, this book is comprehensive and fascinating (upper level).*

Sarquis, Mickey & Jerry Sarquis 1991. *Fun With Chemistry: A Guidebook of K-12 Activities.* Madison, WI: Institute for Chemical Education, University of Wisconsin.

Sae, Andy 1990. "Of Cabbages and Anthocyanins."*The Science Teacher.* October. *An informative article on how you can use red cabbage in your classroom.*

Shakhashiri, Bassam 1989. *Chemical Demonstrations: A Handbook for Teachers of Chemistry, Vol. 3.* Madison, WI: University of Wisconsin Press. *From a teaching star at the University of Wisconsin - Madison.*

Yanagita, Tomomichi 1990. *Natural Microbial Communities: Ecological and Physiological Features.* Tokyo: Japan Scientific Press. *A well-written graduate level text on microbes in soil, water, atmosphere and food.*

Chapter 4

What goes on under your feet?

SOIL MEDITATIONS

Are you walking on air? Think about the earth under your feet. It seems solid. You can jump on it and nothing appears to collapse under you. But if the earth is so solid, where do trees and other plants put their roots? How do earthworms breathe? And why does rainwater soak into the ground?

Soil comes from solid rock that has broken down into very tiny particles, and also from decomposed plant and animal tissues. These bits of rock and organic matter are many different shapes and sizes, so they don't fit solidly together, but contain many tiny spaces.

The open spaces between soil particles are filled with air, water and life. One ounce of soil can contain as much as 250,000 square feet of surface area, or about 6 football fields. Millions of bacteria, fungi, algae, protozoa and nematodes can exist in just a handful of soil (for more on microorganisms see p. 17). Other larger soil residents include earthworms, roots, springtails, seeds, moles, badgers and insect larvae.

The world under your feet is wonderfully diverse and complex. Soils vary greatly, not just between regions, but even from one part of a garden to another. You can see, feel and even smell many different soil characteristics, which in turn tell you something about a soil's chemical and mineral makeup. Factors that influence soils include the types of rock they come from, their age, rainfall and other climatic factors, topography and human activity.

You can use the **Sedimentation Bottle**, the **Soil Column** and other explorations in this chapter to look at many different soil characteristics, including texture and how soil holds water. You can even "cook with soils," and grow plants to test your results.

 **CONNECTIONS:** *microbiology, geology, agriculture, soil ecology, plant nutrition, physics, math, geometry. Scientific process skills – observing, data recording, quantification, inferring, comparing.*

BUILD:

SEDIMENTATION BOTTLE

MATERIALS:

- one 1-liter bottle plus cap
- Bottle Biology Tool Kit (p. 2)
- graduated cylinder or other measured container
- 200 cubic centimeters (ccs) soil
- water

1. Remove the label from a 1-liter bottle (see p. 3).

3. Using a graduated cylinder, or some other known measured container, add water to the bottle in 100 ml increments, marking your bottle every 100 milliliters (or cubic centimeters) from the bottom to the 1000 ml point.

Use a waterproof pen. You'll notice the spacing between marks changes as the bottle changes shape.

2. If your bottle has a base, trim away sides of base to expose entire bottle.

trim off base to expose entire bottle

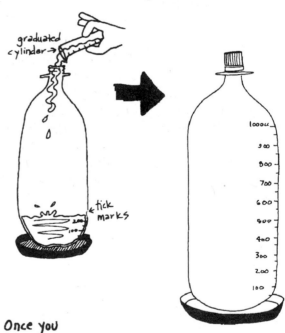

graduated cylinder→

←tick marks

Once you make one bottle you can use it as a guide to make others like it.

FILL

Collecting soil samples: The first step in this series of soil explorations is to collect soil. Collect from at least two different places — backyards, city parks, playgrounds, construction sites, road cuts, woods, or farm fields. Soils are frequently very diverse, so you can collect from different spots in one area and still obtain soils with different characteristics.

Collect at least **600 ccs** (approximately 3 cups) of each type of soil, which will be enough for several experiments. (Solids like soils are measured in cubic centimeters (ccs); milliliters (mls) are reserved for measuring liquids.)

Time for drying: Air dry your samples by spreading them out on newspaper for three to four days. (Don't oven-dry soils since the heat will kill microscopic life and drive off the molecularly-bound water in the clays, fundamentally altering the soil characteristics.) When your samples are dry, you can store them in plastic milk jugs or other airtight containers. Be sure to label each sample according to where it came from.

The Sedimentation Bottle: This project allows you to observe some of the diversity of particles in a handful of soil from your own backyard. By mixing soil and water in a bottle, and then observing the layering of the soil as it settles, you will see differently shaped, sized and colored particles in the soil.

shake vigorously!

Add 200 ccs (1.3 cups) of a sample soil to the Sedimentation Bottle. Fill it with water to the 1000 cc mark. You can also add 2 to 3 mls (half a tsp) of laundry detergent to help disperse the soil particles.

Shake the bottle vigorously and set it someplace where you can watch the soil settle. A windowsill is one good place. Some particles will settle immediately, others will continue to be suspended for days.

OBSERVE

Particle fallout: How many different layers can you identify? After everything has settled, re-shake the bottle and time the settlement rates of the various particles. Can you graph your results?

Some soils may have many fine clay particles that remain suspended in the water for hours or even days. You may also observe a layer of decomposing plant material or organic matter floating on the surface of the water. You will see some of these particles fall slowly as they soak up enough water to sink.

Gas bubbles: Let the bottle sit for a day or two and then tap the sides. Does anything happen? Photosynthesis and respiration by algae and soil bacteria may have produced many tiny gas bubbles, which will rise to the surface when you tap the bottle. You may also see crumbs of soil rising to the surface, buoyed up by gas bubbles produced by soil microbes. What happens if you make two identical soil columns and keep one in a dark place?

Darkle, darkle little grain
I wonder how you entertain
A thousand creatures
     microscopic.
Grains like you from Pole to
     Tropic
Sustain land life on this
     planet!
I marvel at you, crumb of
     granite.

— Francis Hole, 1992
Soil Scientist,
Professor Emeritus
University of Wisconsin,
Madison

BUILD:

Soil Column

MATERIALS:

- two 1-liter bottles
- one cap
- Bottle Biology Tool Kit (p. 2)
- graduated cylinder
- 500 ccs soil
- water

1. Remove labels from two 1-liter bottles. Remove the base from one, if bottle has a separable base.

Bottle #1   Bottle #2

remove base

2. Cut bottle #1 roughly in half, about 13 cm from the bottom.

Bottle #1

approx. 13 cm

A

3. Cut bottom off Bottle #2, 1-2 cm below the hip.

B   Bottle #2

cut 1cm below hip

4. Attach cap to top "B". Invert "B" into "A".

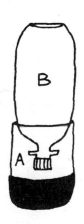

B

A

5. Use a graduated cylinder, or some other known measured container, to mark off the volume of your bottle by 100 ccs (or mls).

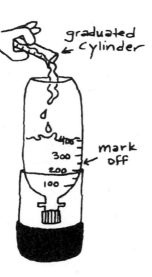

graduated cylinder

400
300
200
100

mark off

6. Empty bottle. Remove cap and poke drainage holes in the cap. Replace.

Use the trimmed top half of Bottle #1 as a top for the Soil Column.

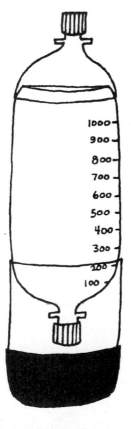

1000
900
800
700
600
500
400
300
200
100

FILL

Soil Column: How much water can your soil hold? **Water holding capacity** is the ability of soil to hold on to moisture against the force of gravity. The ability of a soil to retain water depends in part on the soil's texture (see p. 43).

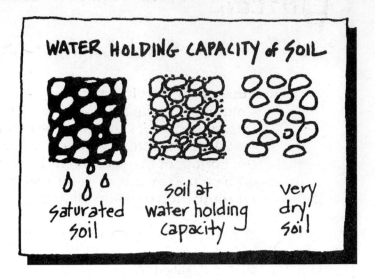

WATER HOLDING CAPACITY of SOIL

saturated soil

soil at water holding capacity

very dry soil

A soil's water holding capacity is important to farmers and gardeners because it indicates how much water is available to plants.

Just add water: Fill the Soil Column with 500 ccs of a sample soil. Add water, 20 mls at a time, until the soil is thoroughly wetted, or when water just begins to drip out of the bottom of the column.

Your soil may contain lots of organic matter, which resists absorbing water. This may cause water to channel through the soil and leave dry areas.

If this happens, thoroughly wet all the soil by stirring the column contents until the soil has been thoroughly moistened. Dump any water that has dripped into the bottom chamber of the column back into the top.

Follow the chart on the next page for directions on determining water holding capacity.

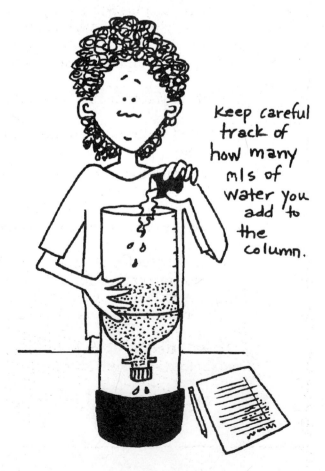

Keep careful track of how many mls of water you add to the column.

► SOIL OBSERVATION CHART ◄

Determine water holding capacity: Thoroughly wet 500 ccs of soil in your Soil Column, keeping careful track of how many mls of water you add. Call this amount W_1. Cover the column to minimize evaporation and let it sit for 24 hours. After 24 hours, measure any water that has drained into the bottom of the column and call it W_2. Subtract W_2 from W_1. The result is the total amount of water now held by the soil in your column, and is an estimation of your soil sample's water holding capacity.

Water added to wet 500 ccs of soil (W_1): _____ mls

Water drained from column after 24 hours (W_2): _____ mls

Total amount of water held by 500 ccs of soil,
or water holding capacity, (W_1 - W_2): _____ mls

Measure soil pH: Test the pH of the water before you pour it through your column and compare that to the pH of the water that drips through your column. For more on pH and how to measure it, see p. 26.

Soils in wetter regions tend to be more acidic, and those in dry regions more alkaline, or basic. This is because water moving through soil tends to carry basic minerals deeper into the soil. The soil surface is then left more acidic. Some soils such as those derived from limestone, however, have a **buffering capacity**. That is, their mineral makeup has a neutralizing effect. This is why lakes in limestone areas are less susceptible to the detrimental effects of acid rain.

pH of water before addition to column: _____

pH of water after running through column: _____

Describe soil changes: Has the soil swelled or settled in your column in response to the water you added? Changes may occur for several days after the initial watering due to certain types of clay and organic materials that swell in the presence of water.

Has the **color** changed in response to moisture? How about **odor**? Let your column sit for a week or two to see if anything grows. Very often any soil you collect will contain plant seeds, moss or fern spores, or even worm cocoons and insect eggs.

Soil height (from bottom of column to soil surface)
before soil saturation: _____ cm

Soil height after ___ hrs or ___ days: _____ cm

Film Can Mysteries: How dense is dirt?

Density: In this exploration, you will fill film cans with several different soil components and soil types, and compare their densities. A soil's density is determined by the type of material it is derived from and how loosely or tightly soil particles are packed.

Collect soil samples and/or soil components such as **gravel**, **sand**, **silt**, **vermiculite**, **clay** and organic matter such as **peat moss**, **compost**, or **manure**. Air dry any samples you collect since moisture content can affect density. You will also need five to eleven **black film cans**.

Completely fill each film can with a sample soil or soil component and snap on the lids. Leave two cans empty. Fill one of the last two cans with **water** and leave the other **empty**. Randomly number all the cans, but keep a list indicating which numbered film can corresponds to which type of soil, soil components, water, or air. You will also need a **Bottle Balance** (p. 115), or another balance to weigh your film cans.

Teacher's note: If you make five or six identical sets of the mystery film cans, you can divide your class into five or six cooperative groups. Group members can take turns weighing, balancing, recording answers and writing their results on the board.

How heavy are they?: Pick up the mystery film cans. Weigh them in your hands. How heavy are they? Shake them next to your ear. What do you hear?

Next, weigh the film cans in your hands and **rank** them from lightest to heaviest. Use the numbers on the lids to identify them, and write a series on the blackboard like this:

2 < 1 < 3 < 6 < 5 < 4

Now you have an idea of how the film cans compare to each other in weight. But how would you figure out the exact density of each film can?

We will estimate the densities of different types of soil by comparing their weights.

We can do this by comparing the same amount, or volume, of different soils. In this case we are using one film can. (Since density equals weight per volume, and we will be using a volume of one film can, the density of the soil will be equal to its weight. *What weighs more, a pound of feathers or a pound of bricks?*)

Using a standard: In order to measure anything, you need a universal standard with which to compare it. In this case you have the convenient standard of water, which has a defined density of **one**. We also know that one film can holds 33 mls of water. Since density equals weight (grams in this case) per volume, we know the film can of water has a density of 33 grams/33 mls.

Find the film can of water. (You can tell by shaking the cans.) Use the bottle balance to determine how your mystery film cans compare to water. Place the film can of water on one side of the balance, and a mystery can on the other side. Does the can of soil weigh more or less than the can of water?

Next, balance the scale. You can determine the difference between the weights of the water and the soil by adding water to the lighter side to balance the scale. Measure exactly how much water you added.

Figuring soil densities: You can now calculate the soil densities. Say you have a soil that is heavier than water. To balance the scale you added 33 mls of water. This means your soil is equal to one film can of water, plus another 33 mls, or a second film can of water.

Your soil, in other words, is equal to two film cans of water, or is twice as dense as water.

To think about this numerically remember that water has a density of 33 grams/33mls, and you had to add 33 grams worth of water to balance the scale. So your mystery film can is equal to 33 grams plus 33 grams, or 66 grams/33 mls. A quick calculation will tell you that this equals **two**.

Continue this exercise with the other mystery film cans in your collection. Afterwards, open the cans and examine the contents. How do the densities compare?

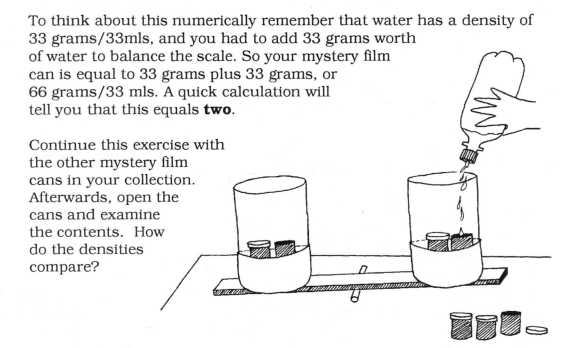

Cooking with Soils : Experiment with plant nutrition

A plant's view of the soil: If you were a plant root, what would soil mean to you? The surrounding soil would provide air to breathe, water to drink, nutrients, and shelter from storms and errant footsteps. In your soil surroundings you would see a diverse world of differently shaped and sized particles. You would see how these particles affect the way water flows, how much water and nutrients are available, and what microorganisms and other soil life you have for company.

You can explore the relationships between plants and soils by growing several plants of the same species under identical conditions but in different soil mixes. Create your own soils by mixing the components of soils that you explored in the Mystery Film Cans section. You can also compare different brands of commercial potting soils.

Create a recipe: Create and record your own soil recipe: equal parts sand, peat moss and garden soil, for example. Mix well and record its properties, including color, feel, water holding capacity and density.

Next, prepare three or four growing systems, (see Gardening Systems for ideas, p. 97). Fill each growing system with your soil recipe, soil samples, or soil components. Record the properties of the samples and components as you did your recipe.

In order to test your recipe, plant several seeds of a fast-growing plant (such as turnip, lettuce, or Wisconsin Fast Plants, see p. 8) in the growing system of each soil component or sample, and in your new soil. Sprout the seeds under exactly the same conditions of light, moisture, temperature, etc. Record the speed of seed germination, rate of plant growth and the general appearance of the plant, including height and the color, size and number of leaves.

How do the plants respond to the different soils? Try using different soil components and different amounts of the components in your recipes. Do all plant species like the same recipes? Experiment and find out. You are searching for the sort of information that helps farmers and gardeners grow the food we eat.

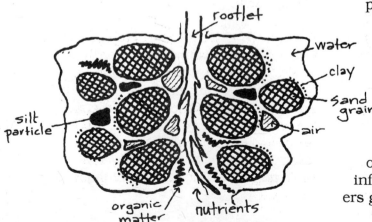

LIFE IN THE ROOT ZONE

What is Soil?
Exploring texture and water holding capacity

While soils vary a great deal, a typical soil is 25% water (unless it has been dried), 45% minerals, 5% organic matter and 25% air.

Soils are made up of variously sized particles, which fall into three basic textures: **sand, silt and clay**. Soils are not usually just sand, silt or clay, but contain all three.

If we could multiply the diameter of a typical sand, silt and clay particle by a thousand, the clay particle would be about as thick as this page, the silt would be about 2.5 cm thick, and the sand about a meter thick!

Soil Particle Size Chart

DIVISION	DIAMETER (mm)
Coarse sand	2.0 - 0.2
fine sand	0.2 - 0.05
Silt	0.05 - 0.002
clay	< 0.002

You can identify a soil's general texture by rubbing a slightly dampened sample between your fingers. If the soil feels gritty and you can see grains, your soil is sandy. If the soil feels smooth and slippery but not really sticky, it is a silty soil. If your sample is very sticky, and you can squeeze it out between your thumb and forefinger into a kind of ribbon, your soil has a high percentage of clay.

Water holding capacity, or how a soil "holds" water, is a function of the size of soil particles. When water enters the soil it moves down, or **percolates**, through soil by flowing through gaps or **pores** between soil particles. The larger the pores, the faster water will move through the soil.

Sandy soil contains larger-sized particles and larger pore spaces, and will drain more quickly. Water percolates more slowly through clay and silt soils because the pores are smaller.

Water also lingers in silt and clay soils because these soils actually hold water by force. Two forces help soil hold onto water: **Adhesion**, which is the attraction between a surface, such as a soil particle, and a water molecule, and **cohesion**, which is the attraction between one water molecule and another.

A soil with more silt and clay particles will bind with water more readily than one with sand particles because the smaller-sized particles offer more soil surface area to which water can adhere. This water will also bind with other water molecules due to cohesion. Silt and clay soils, therefore, have higher water holding capacities than sand.

You might be surprised that smaller particles offer more **surface area**. To bring this concept alive, find two film cans and fill each one with a different size of sphere; marbles in one and dried peas or ball bearings in the other. Which can contains more surface area?

To find out, figure the surface area of the two spheres (surface area = $4\pi r^2$). Then multiply each surface area by the number of peas or marbles you fit into each can. Your answer will show that, within a certain volume, smaller particles offer more surface area than larger particles.

SURFACE AREA =
$4 \pi r^2$

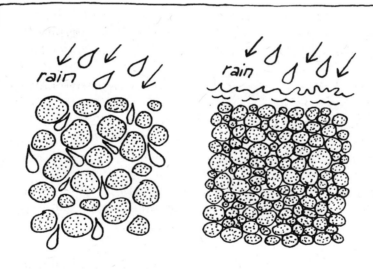

Soils with large pore spaces, such as in sandy soils (left), will usually drain more quickly and have a lower water holding capacity than soils with smaller pore spaces (right). A soil can lose pore space if it is packed down by animals and people or the weight of buildings, for example. Water then flows much more slowly through the soil. Have you every wondered why puddles form under swings after a rainfall?

Additional
Reading

Eswaran, H., T. Kupelian, T. Levermann, & D. Yost 1990. "The Science of Soil." *The Science Teacher.* 57(5): 50-53. *A good, brief intro-duction to soil science and its techniques and tools; includes several lab activities.*

Farb, Peter 1959. *Living Earth.* New York: Harper & Brothers. *A passionate and friendly book written for laypeople interested in learning more about what lives under their feet.*

Fields, Shirley 1993. "Life in a Teaspoon of Soil." *Science Scope.* Febru-ary, p.16. *Elementary-level explorations into a teaspoon of soil to meet the millions that live there.*

Gotsch, Margaret & Shannon Harris 1988. "Soil Lab: Groundwork for Earth Science." *Science Scope* 12 (6): 18-20. *More elementary and middle-school level soil activities.*

Harpstead, M.I., F.D. Hole, & W.F. Bennett 1988. *Soil Science Simpli-fied.* 2nd ed. Ames Iowa: Iowa State University Press. *An excellent introductory soil science text intended for upper-level students.*

Levy, D. & R. Graham 1993. "An Integrative Landscape-Scale Exercise for Introductory Soil Science Classes." *Journal of Natural Resources and Life Sciences Education.* 22 (1): 31-33. *A high school-level soil investigation designed around a 3-hour field trip in which students integrate soil science concepts on a landscape scale.*

"Rooftops of a Hidden World." *EE News.* Spring 1991. DNR Bureau of Information and Education, Madison, WI. *A fun, accessible article introducing the idea of the living soil.*

Yanagita, Tomomichi 1990. *Natural Microbial Communities: Ecological and Physiological Features.* Tokyo: Japan Scientific Societies Press. *A graduate level, well-written text on microbes in soil, water, and atmo-sphere.*

Chapter 5

Who eats whom?

PREDATOR-PREY COLUMN

Animal and plant appearance and behavior is related to a complex set of factors such as climate, availability of nutrients, competition for resources and the presence of disease. Particularly important to understanding how populations of animals and plants look and act, are predator-prey relations — what they eat and what eats them.

Take mimicry, for example, a development in which one species has evolved to look like another poisonous or unappetizing species in order to avoid being eaten. Other evolutionary adaptations include camouflage coloring and thorns for protection, long legs for speed to catch prey or elude a predator, and moving in groups and posting "sentries" to watch for predators.

Besides acting as a tremendous evolutionary force, predator-prey relations also affect an area's ecology. When a bird eats a snail, for example, it transfers energy in a food web.

Predation, or lack of it, can also affect population size.

For example, if a large predator like coyotes becomes rare, then prey populations, such as rabbits, will boom.

With a Predator-Prey Column you can observe the appearance, behavior and interactions of insects, spiders and insect-eating plants.

You can watch insects hatch, feed, molt and maybe even mate. Given their short life cycles and the unnatural conditions in captivity, you are likely to observe death as well.

How does a praying mantis obtain its food? How does a Venus flytrap avoid digesting twigs?

In a Predator-Prey Column you can closely observe two different organisms, learn about the way that they live and how they eat and are eaten.

CONNECTIONS: *food webs, ecosystems, evolution, mutation, selection, natural history, niche, habitat. Scientific process skills — observing, asking questions, making models, classifying, inferring.*

Part One

BUILD: FRUIT FLY TRAP

MATERIALS:

- one 2-liter bottle with base or two 2-liter footed bottles
- one cap
- Bottle Biology Tool Kit (p. 2)
- three to five film cans
- one plastic lid to fit inside base
- small amount of banana or other fruit

1. Remove label and base (if it has a separable base) from a 2-liter bottle (see p. 3).

2. Cut off top 4 cm below shoulder curve.

Cut bottom off 3 cm below hip curve, leaving a tapered end on cylinder.

Save the cap

tapered end

4. Tape top securely so no flies escape. Tape over holes in bottom of base. Place 2-3 slices of banana into 1 film can to start, and set in bottle base. Set the film can on a plastic lid, like that from a cottage cheese container, so it doesn't tip. Once you have caught a few flies, add more film cans loaded with fruit.

3. Punch a 3 to 4 mm hole in cap – just big enough for one fruit fly to pass through at a time. Invert top into cylinder. Set into base. *If you can't find a separate base, you'll need to cut off the lower 9-10 cm of a second footed bottle to act as the base for your trap.*

make fly-sized hole in cap

use base of another bottle if your bottle didn't have one

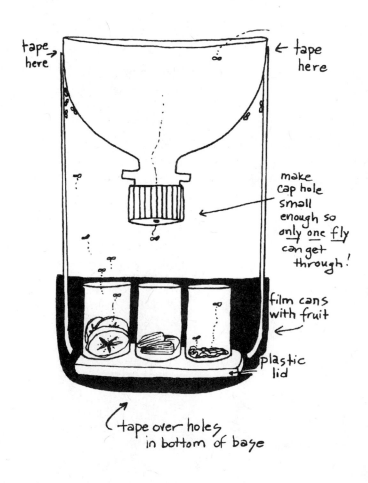

tape here

tape here

make cap hole small enough so only one fly can get through!

film cans with fruit

plastic lid

tape over holes in bottom of base

FILL

The Fruit Fly Trap: To fill a Predator-Prey Column, you need prey. The Fruit Fly Trap allows you to trap wild fruit flies and start a fruit fly colony with which to feed a spider or praying mantis. You can also observe fruit fly development and reproduction. The trap is also a handy way to control fruit flies in your kitchen. It is a good example of environmentally safe and effective pest control.

When, where and how to find fruit flies: Place a few slices of banana, melon or other fruit in a film can in the bottom of your trap. (Once you have trapped several fruit flies you can add more cans of fruit). Odors from the rotting fruit will attract fruit flies *(Drosophila melanogaster)*. They will follow the scent through the hole in the bottom of your trap, but only a few will be able to escape because of the trap's design.

Fruit flies are most common in the summer and autumn, when there are many ripe fruits and vegetables available. You may have trouble luring wild fruit flies, especially in the dead of winter. Try several different locations — outside, in your kitchen and at school. If all else fails, you can obtain fruit flies from lab supply companies (p. 8) or perhaps from a local high school or college science teacher.

Female fruit flies in the trap will lay eggs in the fruit and within a few days eggs will hatch, producing tiny whitish **larvae**. These larvae are very active feeders and will burrow into the fruit and even climb the walls of the film cans and the trap. After several days, the larvae will find a dry location and turn into **pupae**, which in a few more days will hatch into fruit flies.

The speed of the life cycle is affected by temperature; at 24-27 degrees C (approximately 75-80 degrees F), the entire cycle takes 10 - 14 days.

Mold problem?: Watch your fruit closely for the first few days. If you see mold growing, discard the fruit and reset the trap in a new location. (Start with just one can of banana.) The mold is an indication that no fruit flies visited your trap within the first few days after you set it.

moldy fruit and no flies?

When fruit flies land on fruit they introduce yeast spores. This causes the fruit to ferment and lowers the pH. The flies actually feed on the yeast, not the fruit. Since molds do not like acidic environments, the fermentation prohibits mold. Once the mold has started to grow, however, its presence will discourage flies.

Trapping: You may want to trap fruit flies in order to control their numbers rather than to breed them. If this is the case, remove the film cans every four to seven days, or when you can see the larvae in the fruit, and discard the fruit. Put the larvae outside, or flush them down the drain, to make sure you are getting rid of the flies. If you throw them into the trash, chances are the larvae will happily pupate, hatch and start flying around.

Handling: When disturbed, trapped fruit flies will fly upwards and crawl around the sides of the trap. To add or remove film cans, tap the side of the trap, pull off the base, and quickly remove a film can full of larvae. Place other film cans loaded with fresh fruit into the trap in order to breed more flies. By replacing the film cans, or just adding fruit to the cans, you can keep the fruit fly colony thriving.

One way to transfer hatched flies is to place the Fruit Fly Trap in the refrigerator for half an hour. The cold will slow the flies down so you can move them to a Predator-Prey Column.

Fruit fly eating habits: Fruit flies do not actually eat fruit, but live off the yeast growing on fruit. Fruit flies carry yeast spores in their guts and on the pads of their feet, so when they land on fruit, they inoculate it with yeast (introducing the yeast into the fruit). You can tell when fruit flies have visited the fruit because the yeast begins to ferment the fruit, which emits a sharp odor. (This is, by the way, related to the same fermentation that produces beer and wine. For more on fermentation, see p. 23).

To explore this process, place two film cans of fruit in a trap, but cover one with mesh to exclude the flies. Compare the contents after several days. You might also experiment with different kinds of fruit. Do fruit flies have preferences? Do some fruits mold when others do not?

Part Two

BUILD: PREDATOR-PREY COLUMN

MATERIALS:

- two 2-liter soda bottles
- one soda bottle cap
- Bottle Biology Tool Kit (p. 2)
- one to three film cans
- water feeder (see p. 53)
- distilled water for the carnivorous plants
- soil, twigs, small plants
- the prey: fruit flies
- the predator: preying mantises, spiders or carnivorous plants (see lab supply companies, p. 8)

1. Remove labels and bases (if they have separable bases) from two 2-liter bottles, (see p. 2).

2. Cut Bottle #1 2 cm above the shoulder curve, leaving a tapered end on cylinder A. Cut 1 cm below the hip curve, leaving another tapered end on cylinder A.

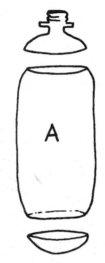

Bottle #1

3. Cut second bottle 0.5 cm below the shoulder curve, leaving a straight end on piece B. Cut bottom off 6 cm above hip curve, leaving a straight side on piece C. Poke a 3 to 4 mm hole in cap and put on piece B. An awl or hot nail poke works well for this (p. 6).

Bottle #2

4. Slide piece B into cylinder A (you may need to work B back and forth to push it all the way in). Set A and B into bottle base D. *If you don't have a separate base use the lower 9-10 cm from a footed bottle.* Piece C serves as a top. Poke air holes. Insert water feeder (see instructions on p. 53).

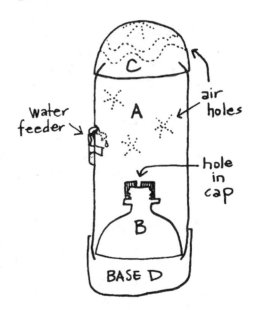

5. Soil, plants and insects will go into the top chamber A, and the film cans of fruit in the base D below. See the Fill section on the following page for instructions.

FILL

Carnivorous Plants

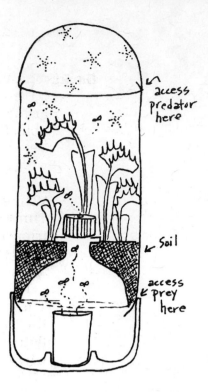

access predator here

Soil

access prey here

Venus flytraps, sundews, and butterworts:
These are a few of the more common carnivorous plants. You can obtain a variety of these plants from lab supply companies (p. 8). You can often buy Venus flytraps at discount stores and garden centers.

Soil: Many carnivorous plants are native to boggy areas with acidic soils. Try growing them in a sand and peat mixture with a little bit of soil. To help moderate the pH, add a small amount of activated charcoal, which you can find at garden, pet or fish supply stores.

Moisture and temperature: Venus flytraps and sundew plants prefer a very humid environment, so keep the soil moist. Water should regularly condense on the sides of the column. If, however, lots of algae begins to grow on the soil surface and the leaves of the plants begin to blacken, conditions may be too moist. Poke more air holes!

Butterworts prefer a better drained soil. To create drier conditions, poke a few drainage holes in the nested bottle top inside the column (part B), before adding soil. All carnivorous plants prefer *distilled*, or *demineralized*, water.

Venus Flytrap

Light and food: Soda bottles become steambaths very easily. *Keep the columns out of direct sunlight* in order to avoid overheating the contents. These plants do need light, however, so if your classroom lacks windows, or has only small ones, you might use a Grow Bucket (see p. 105).

Carnivorous plants will struggle along without insect food, but just a few insects will help them grow vigorously. Feed your plants with just one film can's worth of breeding fruit flies, and experiment with feeding them more or less. You don't want to overwhelm the bottle with too many fruit flies.

Venus flytraps can grow too large to hold fruit flies. Watch them carefully to see that they close tightly enough to trap fruit flies. If not, feed them houseflies or other larger insects.

Background: Carnivorous plants obtain necessary nutrients from insects. A large number of these plants live in boggy areas where the soil is highly acidic, and important nutrients such as nitrogen are not readily available. (This is why you should not fertilize carnivorous plants.) The Venus flytrap *(Dionaea sp.)*, the sundew *(Drosera sp.)*, and the butterwort *(Pinguicula sp.)*, all trap and digest insects to obtain nitrogen.

Venus flytraps have clam-shell shaped leaves that act like spring traps. Three tiny trigger hairs line each half of the trap. When these hairs are tripped by an ant or fly, pressurized cells that hold the leaf halves apart suddenly lose their pressure and the two halves swing shut within about a second, trapping the insect between them.

These hairs must be touched twice within about 30 seconds to trigger the trap. A raindrop or falling twig won't cause the leaf to close. Venus flytraps also have "tasting" glands inside their leaves which determine whether they have trapped something worth digesting.

Water Feeder

You can make the water feeder out of any small plastic container. Those that work best include small candy containers like the type that hold breath mints, syringe holders (free from veterinarians) and plastic microcentrifuge tubes (cheap from lab supply companies, see p. 8).

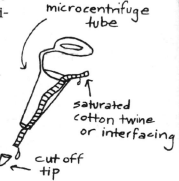

For the wick, cut a short piece of cotton twine, a strip of a utility wipe or a strip of fabric interfacing available from fabric supply stores. You should first wash the interfacing and utility wipes to remove detergents, flame retardants and other substances. Wet this wick thoroughly with water, and then insert it into the plastic container you are using for a feeder.

If you use a microcentrifuge tube or a syringe holder, cut off the very tip, insert the wick, and then place the tube into a hole poked in the top of your Predator-Prey Column. Otherwise, attach the container to the column with a rubber band or a piece of tape, and feed the wick through a small hole in the side of the column. Take care poking the hole in the column, so the space around the container or wick isn't so big that fruit flies or other column contents can escape. *Keep the water feeder full of water at all times!*

If the leaf has closed on something indigestible, it will reopen within a few hours. The individual leaves on a Venus flytrap function as a trap only once, however, although they may reopen after digesting an insect.

The tiny leaves of the insect-eating **sundew** plant are covered in long tentacle-like hairs, at the ends of which sit drops of sweet and sticky liquid. Insects are attracted and then caught in the clear liquid. As the insect struggles, the leaf hairs bend inward so the leaf curves around the insect. The plant then secretes enzymes through the hairs, which digest its prey.

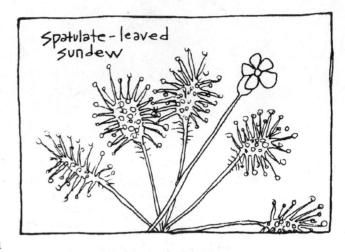

Spatulate-leaved sundew

The **butterwort** has numerous glands scattered over its leaves, some of which exude a sticky liquid, making the leaf like living fly paper. An ant or fly struggling to release itself triggers other glands on the leaf that pour out digestive enzymes. These enzymes pool around the unfortunate insect, digest it, and then soak into the leaf carrying the nutrients to the rest of the plant.

FILL

PRAYING MANTIS

Although you can
capture mature mantises
in the wild or order them
full-grown from lab supply
companies, we recommend raising
them from an egg case. You can purchase an egg case from a lab supply company (see p. 8). Store the case in the refrigerator,
where it will keep for many months. When you are
prepared to raise mantises, take the egg case out of the
refrigerator and put it in a Predator-Prey Column at room
temperature.

Timing is everything: Before an egg case hatches be sure that you have a steady supply of fruit flies to feed the hatchlings. (See Fruit Fly Trap in this chapter.) If you can't find any wild fruit flies, order some from a lab supply company (p. 8).

You will also need to make several Predator-Prey Columns in which to put your young mantises, depending on how many you want to raise.

After two to six weeks, hundreds of tiny mantises will pour out of the egg case. *The hatchlings must have water within the first 12 hours*, so keep a moist wick in the cage during the last weeks before hatching. As long as the mantises are in the same bottle, and especially without another source of food, they will eat each other. It is also quite common for many mantises to die during these early stages.

Fill your Predator-Prey Columns with soil, a plant for moisture and a twig or two so the mantises can climb to the top of the column to reach the water feeder and fruit flies. Place one or two young mantises in each column with one to three canisters of breeding fruit flies below. Release the other mantises outside.

Food: The rate at which your mantises will grow depends in part on how much you feed them. (It is very difficult to overfeed a praying mantis.) Mantises will eat only live food. In general, it's a good idea to keep a daily supply of food available, and to feed mantises heavily before weekends. Keep the water feeder full at all times.

Your mantises will eventually outgrow the fruit flies. (It will be like keeping an elephant alive on peanuts.) At this point you can feed the mantises a variety of common insects such as house flies, crickets and roaches. If you don't have any expert fly catchers around, you can obtain crickets from lab supply companies (p. 8) and pet stores.

Growth: Mantises typically grow to be 7 to 10 cm long. As they grow, they periodically shed their outer skin when it becomes too small and a new, larger outer skin has developed underneath. Mantises **molt**, as this process is called, approximately half a dozen times. They develop long wings in their final molt, which signifies they are full grown and ready to mate.

NOTE! Mantises are very vulnerable just before, during, and for a few hours after a molt. Large crickets and other mantises will eat a molting, and basically defenseless, mantis. To be safe, never leave uneaten crickets in a bottle with a mantis.

Where to keep them: Mantises do well at room temperature. Beware of sunny or drafty window sills.

In the wild: The praying mantis has been called the tiger of the insect world for good reason. Watching a mantis sight, stalk, then seize an oblivious fly is a thrilling and chilling experience. You will need to provide captive mantises with lots of food, but they will reward you with plenty of activity.

Mantises obtain their food in the wild by sitting in bushes or grass and waiting for a cricket or fly to come to them. The female mantises are distinguishable from males by much larger abdomens. Mantises mate in late summer, and fertilized females can lay 15 or more cases, each containing hundreds of eggs.

You may find egg cases, which look like masses of hard, tan foam, one to three inches long, on twigs and stems in open fields in many parts of the U.S. The egg cases hatch in the late spring. The hatchlings molt several times during the summer and emerge from a final molt as a mature adult with developed wings. At this point they are ready to mate.

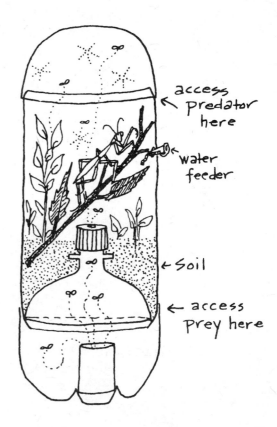

access predator here

water feeder

← Soil

← access prey here

FILL

SPIDERS

Spiders come in all shapes and sizes. There are some 35,000 species worldwide. Spiders are not insects, but belong to a group called the **Arachnids**. The name comes from a Greek myth about an expert weaver named Arachne who challenged the goddess Athena to a weaving contest. Athena lost, and her irritation at being out-woven drove her to change Arachne into a spider. While not all spiders weave webs, they all have eight legs, and all eat insects.

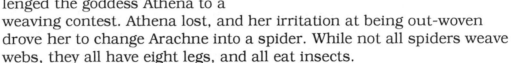

Spiders in bottles: The most successful types of spiders for Predator-Prey Columns are very small, web-building spiders. You will find them in windows, around porches and in garages and corners of rooms at home or school. You may find spiders of many sizes, but choose only the smallest for your bottle.

If, after 24 hours your spider has not built a web and does not appear to be settling into its new bottle habitat, let it free and try another spider. Spiders also live quite happily at large in a classroom. They help to control populations of fruit flies, especially near Decomposition Columns.

You can also try hatching spiders from an egg sac. Female spiders create egg sacs at the end of the summer, and can frequently be found hanging in webs in windows. Put a sac carefully in a bottle, hanging from a twig. In the right conditions, the sac will hatch within one to two months. You will then see hundreds of tiny spiders crawling around looking for some place to set up a home. Let most of the babies go, but keep a few for your columns.

Habitat: Your spider will need a stick or twig, set diagonally in the column and reaching just to the rim, from which to spin its web. Small plants living in the bottle of the column will provide the habitat with some moisture. Keep a full water feeder in the column as well.

Handling: Spiders are easy to transport, either sitting directly on a twig you offer them to climb onto, or hanging from a thread of their own silk.

Beck, Charles 1992. "Are You as Clever as a Spider?" *Science Scope* 16(2): 12-16. *A middle school-level web-building activity.*

Foelix, Ranier 1982. *Biology of Spiders.* Cambridge, Massachusetts: Harvard University Press. *A graduate-level, in-depth text on spiders.*

Frost, Samuel 1959. *Insect Life and Insect Natural History.* New York: Dover Publications. *An older book intended as an introduction to insect studies for adults. Well-written chapters on general aspects of insect life include sonification, insect-plant relationships and social behavior.*

Hanif, Muhammad 1990. "The Vanishing Bog." *Science and Children,* 27(7): 25-27. *More information on creating a good home for carnivorous plants.*

Hopf, Alice 1990. *Spiders.* New York: E.P. Dutton. *Great introduction for anyone interested in spiders. Upper-level elementary.*

Johnson, S.A. 1984. *Mantises.* Minneapolis: Lerner Publications. *An elementary-level introduction to the tiger of the insect world.*

Settel, Joanne and Nancy Baggett 1986. *How Do Ants Know When You're Having A Picnic? (and other questions kids ask about insects and other crawly things).* New York: Atheneum. *This book contains answers to questions kids and adults ask about ants, bees, lice, flies, spiders, ticks, moths, snails and other creatures.*

Stokes, Donald 1983. *A Guide to Observing Insect Lives.* Boston: Little, Brown and Company. *A friendly, practical guide to watching the drama of insect life all around us, and throughout the year.*

Wilkins, Malcolm 1988. *Plantwatching: How Plants Remember, Tell Time, Form Partnerships and More.* New York: Facts on File Publications. *You will never take a plant for granted after reading this book! Beautifully illustrated and well-researched and written. Upper-level.*

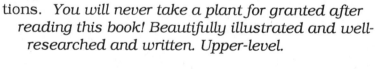

NOTES

Chapter 6

What is the land-water connection?
TERRAQUA COLUMN

What common substance falls from the atmosphere, flows through our bodies, runs through the soil beneath our feet, collects in puddles and lakes, then vaporizes back into the atmosphere in a never-ending cycle?

Water, as it cycles between land, ocean and atmosphere, forms the major link between the terrestrial world (involving anything living on the earth) and the aquatic world (involving anything living on or in the water).

Water drips off rooftops, flows over roads, off your toothbrush, and down the drain, percolates through the soils of fields and forests and eventually finds its way into rivers, lakes and oceans.

During its journey, water will pick up leaf litter, soil, nutrients, agricultural chemicals, road salts and gasoline from cars, all of which have profound impacts on life in aquatic systems. Water can also be filtered or purified as it percolates through soil.

The TerrAqua Column (TAC) provides you with a model to explore the link between land and water. The model has three basic components: soil, water and plants.

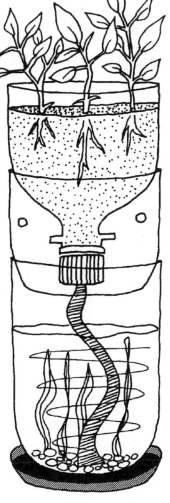

By varying the treatment of just one of these components you can explore how one variable can affect the whole system. How does salt affect the growth of plants? How does adding fertilizer to the soil affect algal growth in the water chamber? What type of soil best purifies water?

Experimentation with the TAC is practically unlimited. You can define a question, then design your own experiment to explore it.

 **CONNECTIONS:** *terrestrial and aquatic systems, water cycle, land-use and water quality, point-source pollution, ecology, soil science, agriculture. Scientific process skills — making observations, designing experiments, recording and analyzing data, making models, inferring.*

MATERIALS:

- two 2-liter bottles
- one bottle cap
- Bottle Biology Tool Kit (p. 2)
- wicking material — *fabric interfacing or cotton string*
- water, soil & plants

1. Remove labels from the two bottles. Remove base from one bottle, if they both have separable bases (see Bottle Basics p. 3).

2. Cut the bottle with no base, 6-7 cm below shoulder curve, leaving a straight end on cylinder B.

Cut off the bottom 1-2 cm below hip curve, leaving a tapered end on cylinder B.

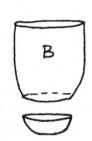
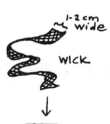

3. Cut top off second bottle 2 cm below shoulder, leaving a straight end on piece C.

4. Punch or drill a hole in cap with an awl or drill. It is very important to enlarge the hole with a tapered reamer or drill bit to about 1 cm wide, enough to easily accommodate the wick. Attach cap to A.

5. Invert top A into cylinder B. Tape this joint for stability. Slide A/B unit into C.

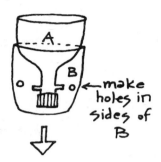

← make holes in sides of B

6. For wick, cut a strip of fabric interfacing 1-2 cm wide and slightly shorter than the height of the column. Insert a wet wick as shown.

cut away base for better viewing.

1-2 cm wide

WICK

WATER

Saturate wick in water, then insert into column, threading through cap.

When adding soil, make sure the wick runs up into the soil and is not plastered along the sides of the column or protruding above the soil surface. After you fill the column you may want to tape B and C together.

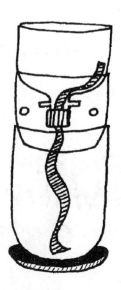

FILL

What goes in a TAC?: The basic components of the TerrAqua Column are soil, water and plants. How do these components interact in a TerrAqua system? (The word **system** indicates you are dealing with a diversity of organisms and the interactions between them.)

Plants growing in the upper part of the TAC take nutrients from the surrounding soil and, with the aid of the wick, take water and other substances from the aquatic portion below. Substances you add to the terrestrial section will move down, or **percolate**, through the soil and drain into the aquatic section.

How do land and water interact in your area?: Does runoff from fertilized lawns or agriculture threaten the quality of your streams or groundwater? Is salt pollution a problem, from either road salt, irrigation, or saltwater intrusion? Are landfills affecting local groundwater?

Soil, water, and plants: Fill the top unit of your TAC with soil you collect, or with potting soil from a gardening store. Fill the lower aquatic unit with tap water, or water from a pond, lake, puddle or fish tank.

Collected soil and water will likely contain algae, phytoplankton, plant seeds and insect larvae. Store-bought soil and tap water will include far fewer organisms. (To observe this, fill one TAC with soil and water from nearby woods or park and another with potting soil from a garden store and tap water. Set them side by side and observe for several weeks. For more on soil life, refer to "Soil Meditations," p. 33.)

Terrestrial and aquatic plants are excellent indicators of change in your system. Fast-germinating and fast-growing plants will most effectively register change in a short period of time.

Grasses, particularly lawn seed mixes, work well. Prairie grasses grow more slowly but have deep roots that are interesting to observe. Radishes and beans also work well, though you will need to soak dried beans overnight before planting. Wisconsin Fast Plants, which have been developed to complete their life cycle in 35-40 days, are ideal candidates for experimentation in TACs (see p. 8).

the Water Cycle

Condensation

Transpiration

Evaporation

Precipitation

Collection

Percolation

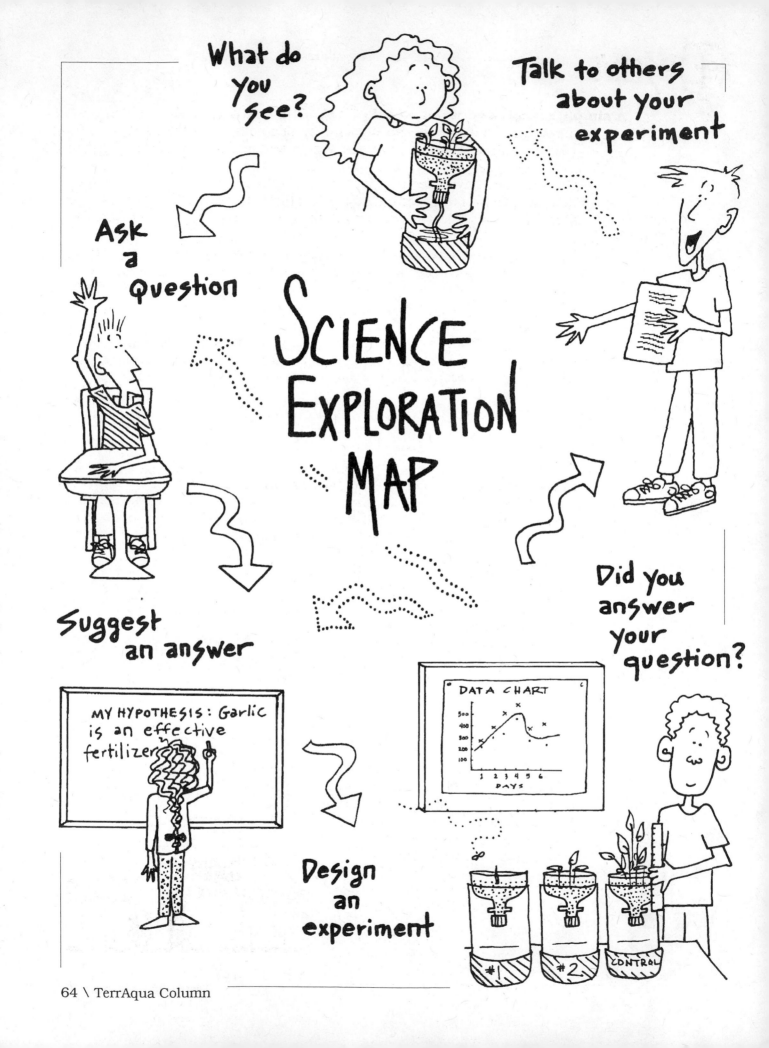

A simple model, a complex world: The TAC, a relatively simple model, allows you to focus on specific aspects of a complex world. Imagine, for example, a lake near your house that is suddenly overtaken with algae.

Given all the environmental factors that influence the lake, you would be hard pressed to determine exactly which factors encouraged the slimy green stuff to get out of control.

You could build several TACs in order to explore specific factors that might encourage algae. Try taking samples of lake water and local soil, for example, and then testing them under different conditions to see in what sorts of environments algae grows best.

Your observations and experiments can go in many directions, so the clearer you are in defining your question and designing your experiment, the more successful your experiment will be.

Variables: Variables to consider in your experiments include:

• The type and amounts of soil, water, and plants – remember, depending on their source, the soil and water will likely contain such life as algae, fungus, mites, *Daphnia,* etc.

• Substances that might affect terrestrial and aquatic systems – nutrients (fertilizers), or pollutants (salts, pesticides, acids).

• A treatment plan – once you have decided on a substance to test you can apply different amounts of that substance; treat only the terrestrial chamber; treat only the water reservoir; apply it directly to plant leaves; test it on plants of various ages, or vary the treatment schedule.

You can fill your TAC with soil you collect from your area.

• Physical factors – temperature, light, sound, etc. (Try singing or screaming at your plants. One student grew Wisconsin Fast Plants to the tunes of Bach, Barry Manilow and Heavy Metal — Barry Manilow encouraged the most growth!!)

Indicators: Indicators in a TAC are plants and animals and other system characteristics that change in response to your experiments, giving you information regarding your hypothesis. Indicators include terrestrial and aquatic plants and the pH of soil and water.

Some observations you can make of a plant indicator, for example, include percentage of seeds that germinate, plant height and weight, leaf size and shape, root structure, number of flowers, length of life cycle and seed production. In the aquatic system, indicators include increases or decreases in populations of algae and duckweed. These changes can show up as cloudiness in the water. You can also use the **bioassay** to determine the effects of a substance on plants (see p. 93).

Controls: With every experiment you run, set up one control TAC in which you do not vary any of the components. This acts as a standard against which you can compare the effects of variables you do change.

Keep it simple: The TAC is a simple model, but all of its parts are dynamic. Keep your investigations very simple by changing only one variable of the system at a time.

Some of the more often investigated substances include fertilizer, pesticides, acid "rain" and oil. A detailed example of a salt pollution experiment follows; you can also use the procedure to investigate other substances.

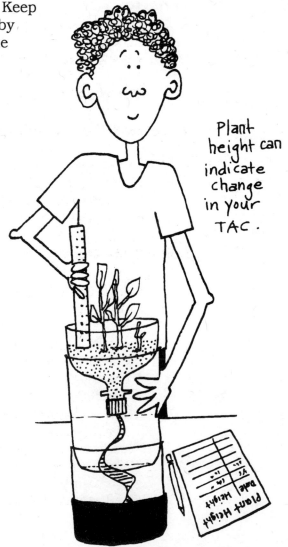

Plant height can indicate change in your TAC.

EXPLORE

Salt Pollution: Does salt affect plant growth?

Roads in Massachusetts* are salted in the winter to de-ice them, frequently with NaCl (sodium chloride), sometimes with $CaCl_2$ (calcium chloride). The question arises whether the salt, carried by melt-water runoff from the road, affects plants growing in the vicinity, or aquatic systems where the runoff goes. The following list of questions and answers provides you with a model for how you might set up an experiment with TACs.

What question are you exploring?

Are plants affected by runoff from roads de-iced with salt in the winter?

What specific idea (hypothesis) are you testing?

Higher concentrations of salt (NaCl) negatively affect plant growth.

What variable will you change in your experiment?

The concentration of NaCl in water fed to plants.

What variables will remain constant in your experiment?

Type of soil, water, and plants, age of plants, and salt treatment schedule. Physical conditions such as temperature and light.

List all the items you will need:

- 4 TACs filled with 50 ml of water below and equal amounts of a potting soil above
- seeds of grass, Wisconsin Fast Plants, radishes, or other fast-growing plants
- 4 labels
- salt – Use road salt, lab grade NaCl, pickling or kosher salt. Table salt often contains iodine and "flowing agents" which may affect results
- eye dropper
- soil testing kit to monitor soil pH (optional)

*Whitney Hagins and Judith Noble and their classes at Medfield High School in Medfield, MA designed this experiment on salt pollution.

What is your experimental procedure?

1. Plant seeds in 4 TACs.

2. After plants have sprouted, label one column CONTROL, label a second 0.1% NaCl, a third 1.0% NaCl and the last TAC 5.0% NaCl.

3. Prepare salt solutions of 0.1%, 1.0% and 5.0% salt by weight. (For example, 0.1% is one tenth of a gram per 100 mls of water, or 1 gram per liter of water.)

4. Treat each TAC with 10 ml of the appropriate salt solution. Use an eye dropper to place 5 ml on the soil and 5 ml in the reservoir. Treat the CONTROL with plain water.

5. Treat plants every fourth day for a month.

6. Observe and record plant development, including height, leaf number, size and color. You might also take pictures of the plants to monitor changes in color and other aspects of physical appearance.

7. Test the soil pH (see p. 26).

8. Repeat this experiment, or run several at once. Can you reproduce your results?

Do the results of your experiment support your hypothesis?

The Medfield High School students found that the higher salt concentrations had more negative effects on plant growth and development.

Discuss your experience with others. Write a report and create a graph to illustrate your investigation.

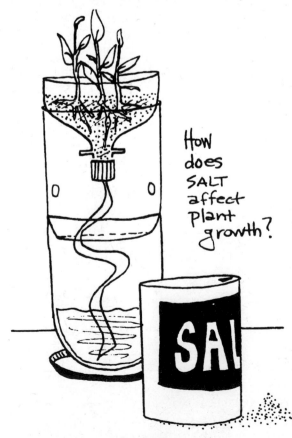

How does SALT affect plant growth?

Water Cycle Column: Is rain pure?

Going with the flow: The Water Cycle Column models some of the ways water moves through natural systems. With this activity you can explore the water cycle and how water and the atmosphere are polluted and purified. Think about the role the water cycle plays in purifying polluted water. What role do plants and soil have in the process?

How it works: Through **capillary action**, water moves up the wick from the bottom unit of the Water Cycle Column into the soil. From there it **evaporates** and becomes **water vapor** in the central chamber. Water vapor also exits from plants growing in the column through **transpiration**, caused by the evaporation of water from the leaves of plants.

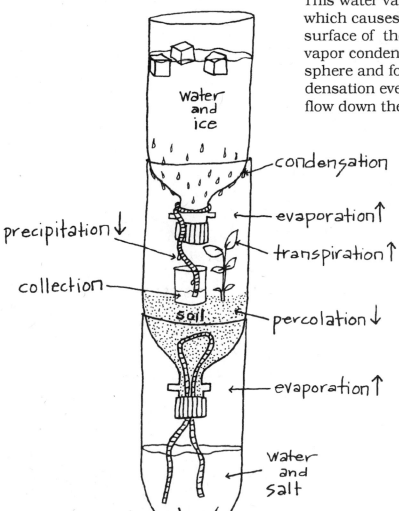

This water vapor is cooled by the ice above, which causes it to **condense** onto the cold surface of the inverted bottle, just as water vapor condenses around particles in the atmosphere and forms clouds. These drops of condensation eventually run down the bottle and flow down the string. This is **precipitation**.

Precipitating water **collects** in the film can, just as water falling as rain or snow collects in ponds, lakes and oceans.

How might you test the purity of the water that "rained" into the film can? Turn the page to build your own Water Cycle Column and to find out more.

BUILD: WATER CYCLE COLUMN

MATERIALS:

- three 1- or 2-liter bottles
- two bottle caps
- 60 cm heavy cotton string for a wick
- one clear 35 mm film can
- Bottle Biology Tool Kit (p. 2)
- soil, water, ice, moss and plant seeds – turnips, Chinese cabbage, Wisconsin Fast Plants (p. 8)

1. Remove labels from bottles (see p. 3).

2. Cut Bottle #1 just below shoulder so a straight edge remains on the cylinder.

Bottle #1

3. Cut Bottles #2 & #3 just above hips, or above black bases, so cylinders have straight sides.

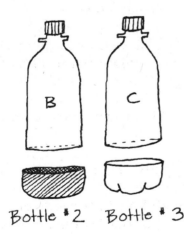

Bottle #2   Bottle #3

4. Poke a hole in one cap. Place cap on B. Insert a loop of string (about 40 cm), so about 5 cm hangs down from cap.

5. Place cap with no hole on C. Tie about 20 cm of string around bottle neck so one end hangs down about 7 cm.

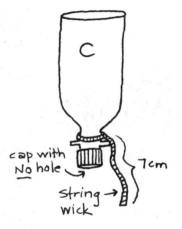

cap with No hole

7cm

string wick

6. Assemble column as shown.

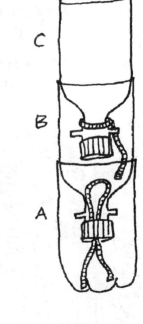

Place string wick in bottle B

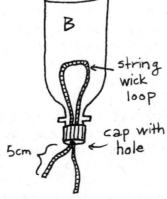

string wick loop

cap with hole

5cm

FILL

Add water, soil and plants: Thoroughly wet both wicks (to read about capillarity see p. 98). Add about 150 mls of water to A. This will be your source of water for the cycle.

Fill B with enough premoistened soil to cover the loop of string (about 200 ccs or 1 cup). The string wick should run up into the soil and *not* be pressed against side of column.

Plant two or three seeds of a fast-growing plant, such as Chinese cabbage or turnip, in the soil around the perimeter of chamber B. When you aren't using the column, leave the top chamber off so that air circulates and your seeds can sprout and grow.

Place the film can on top of the soil in the center of B, so that the wick from C hangs into it. Trim the film can, or use a bottle cap, if a full-sized film can will not fit between the top chamber and the soil.

Fill C with ice water, or fill it with water and freeze it.

EXPLORE

Does salt travel?: Add a few grams of salt to the water in the column's bottom chamber. Will the water that eventually "rains" into the film can be salty? Why isn't water evaporated from the ocean salty?

Add other contaminants to the water or soil. How can you determine if the "rainwater" or soil becomes polluted? (You might plant a bit of moss in the film can to use as an indicator of water purity.)

Heat source: What happens if you put a source of heat near the column, such as an incandescent light?

Make acid rain: Tape a piece of pH paper (see pp 26-27) to the inside of middle chamber B. Tape another to the outside of the bottle. Moisten the papers with a drop of water. Poke a small hole in the side of B. Dip the end of a piece of string into sulphur powder (available from drug, hardware, or garden stores or lab supply companies, p. 8).

Light this same string end on fire briefly and then blow it out so the string smolders. Quickly insert the smoking end through the hole in B for a few seconds. Tape the hole closed and watch the color of the indicator papers. What happens? *Use caution whenever working with burning materials.*

Burning sulphur produces sulphur dioxide, a by-product of burning coal associated with acid rain. How will acid rain affect plants, soil and water in your bottle?

Branley, Franklin 1982. *Water For the World*. New York: T.Y. Crowell. *An elementary-level book describing the water cycle and sources of water, with a few experiments.*

Breit, Frank 1987. "Graphing is Elementary." *Science and Children*, 24(8): 20-22. *A useful, accessible framework for teaching description, quantification, and graphing.*

Cobb, Vicki 1986. *The Trip of a Drip*. Boston: Little, Brown & Co. *An elementary-level book discussing the water cycle from the sink to the ocean.*

Cowing, Sheila 1980. *Our Wild Wetlands*. New York: Julian Messner. *A middle school-level book on how wetlands work.*

Cruzan, John 1988. "Teaching Ecology with Microcosms." *The American Biology Teacher* 50(4): 226-228.

Koker, Mark 1991. "Investigating Groundwater." *Science Scope*, 14(8): 10-15. *A middle school-level introduction into parts-per-million, designed by the Chemical Education for Public Understanding Program.*

McCombs, Laurence and Rosa Nichola 1986. *What's Ecology?* New York: Addison-Wesley.

Postel, Sandra 1989. *Water for Agriculture: Facing the Limits*. Washington, D.C.: Worldwatch Paper 93.

Runyon, Charles 1989. "Does the Acid Rain Hypothesis Hold Water?" *The Science Teacher* 56(3): 30-32.

Vandas, Steve 1992. "How Do We Treat Our Wastewater?" *Science and Children*, 29(8): 18-19. *An elementary level article on the water treatment process -—includes a poster.*

NOTES

Chapter 7

Model your own ecosystem

ECOCOLUMN

Think about all the non-human life with which you share your world. What sorts of insects inhabit your house or your garden outside? What kinds of plants grow near your school or in cracks in the sidewalk?

More specifically, how do these neighbors of yours make a living? Do they build homes? How much space do they need?

What do the spiders in your windows eat? Are there different types of plants competing for space outside your apartment building, or in the park? Where do the fish swimming in a nearby pond or river get their food?

With an Ecocolumn you can design bottle habitats for some of the animals and plants with which you live. You can create homes for spiders, snails, fruit flies, fungi and all sorts of microscopic organisms, and many types of plants.

The Ecocolumn builds on what you have learned in previous chapters in this book. It consists of various interconnected units that you design, construct and fill.

For example, feed your banana peels to a decomposition unit in order to grow some yeast organisms and breed fruit flies, which will feed spiders living in a unit above.

Water the system from the top, and have the water filter through a purifying soil unit and drip into an aquarium at the bottom. The design possibilities are limited only by your imagination.

Before building a column, brainstorm about how to create and maintain habitats. The Niche Kit (p. 81) will give you ideas about habitats and help you think about how to model them in an Ecocolumn.

 **CONNECTIONS:** *ecosystems, energy, water and nutrient cycling, food webs, adaptation, predation, symbiosis, competition, water chemistry, life cycles, niches, decomposition. Scientific process skills — making observations, recording data, asking questions, making models, project design, experimentation.*

BUILD:

ECOCOLUMN

MATERIALS:

- two or more 2-liter bottles of the same brand, with caps
- Bottle Biology Tool Kit (see p. 2)
- soil, water, plants, compost, fruit flies, spiders, snails and other life from small habitats

1. Remove labels from 2 two-liter bottles, and base from one (if it has a separable base; see p. 3).

2. Cut top off Bottle #1 about 1 cm below shoulder. Cut the bottom off 1 cm below hip.

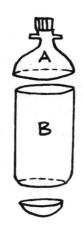

3. Cut top off Bottle #2 about 1 cm below shoulder.

4. Slide A down into B. You now have a stackable unit. Tape A/B joint from underneath. If unit is to hold water, silicone seal inner joint (see p. 7). Stack chamber on C.

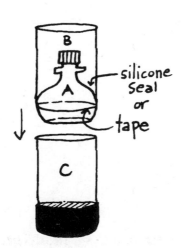

silicone seal or tape

5. Make as many chambers as you need for your stack of habitats. Connect them by punching holes in the caps and bottle tops. See illustrations below and on the following pages for ideas on filling the column. Tape all chambers that need not be opened.

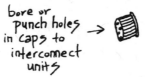

bore or punch holes in caps to interconnect units →

- precipitation funnel
- air holes
- plant or animal habitat
- drainage holes
- porthole
- space units apart using a cylinder with one straight and one tapered end
- soil or decomposition unit
- aquarium

FILL

Your experience in previous chapters in this book will help you fill an Ecocolumn. You can easily integrate a TerrAqua Column, p. 61, a Soil Column, p. 33, a Decomposition Column, p. 11, or a Predator-Prey Column, p. 47 into any Ecocolumn.

The following list of suggestions will help you plan, fill and integrate chambers. Keep in mind that an Ecocolumn can be a long-term project. Students should be prepared to take columns home to care for them over any vacation periods.

Precipitation: Punch two or three small holes in the cap of a bottle top funnel in order to "water" your Ecocolumn. *Note: you can also cap your Ecocolumn using a bottle top or base in order to make a closed system.*

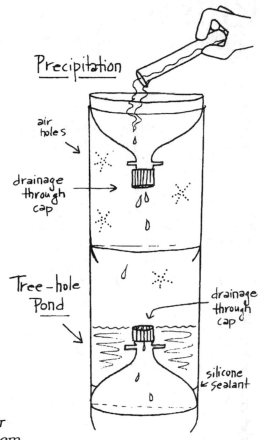

Precipitation

air holes

drainage through cap

Tree-hole Pond

drainage through cap

silicone sealant

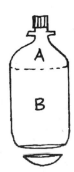

- Version E-Z -

Some teachers prefer a different version of the Ecocolumn "chamber," because the bottle top A nests more easily into cylinder B. Its disadvantage is that water tends to leak out the joint at the bottom because the cylinder's tapered end is at the top. We don't recommend using this version until you have tried the other method or are building an Ecocolumn which will not need to hold water and in which water is not flowing between chambers.

1. Cut top off a 2-liter bottle 2 cm below shoulder. Cut bottom off 2 cm below hip.

2. Invert B and place on top of A. Tape joint.

tapered end on top

tape here

Air holes: Poke plenty of air holes for the living creatures inside. You will need to keep the holes small so that fruit flies do not escape. In aquarium chambers be sure air holes are made well above desired water levels.

Aquariums and tree-hole ponds: A **tree hole pond** is basically a tiny "pond" held by a plant, and the aquatic community that water supports. Small pockets in trees where two limbs come together, for example, can fill with rainwater or snow melt and support a diversity of life including beetle, fly and mosquito larvae and many microbes. These "ponds" can also occur in pitcher plants, bromeliads, hollow bamboo stems and other plants that hold water.

Make this chamber watertight (see p. 7). Fill with water and aquatic life such as snails, algae, duckweed and water insects. Remember that the aquarium's chemistry will be greatly affected by any water dripping in from units above. The pond can drain through small holes poked in the cap, which will also water the chamber below.

Decomposing fruit and breeding fruit flies:
Fill a decomposition unit with plant matter and include a small amount of fruit in which fruit flies are breeding (see the Decomposition Column, p. 11, and the Fruit Fly Trap, p. 48). A porthole cut in the side will allow you to add more compost to feed your fruit fly colony. Cover the hole with a piece from another bottle, hinged with a wide piece of tape. The door should fit tightly so fruit flies don't escape. Poke holes in the cap at the bottom of the decomposition unit or leave the cap off so that water can drain.

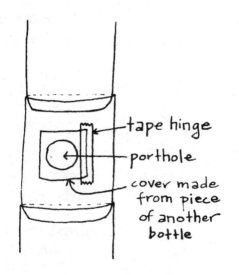

tape hinge
porthole
cover made from piece of another bottle

Spiders, mantises and other predators: Above the fruit fly breeder you can create a habitat for a predator such as a praying mantis, a spider or a carnivorous plant (see Predator-Prey Column p. 52). Fill it with soil, plants and a twig or two in order to give your predator a good home.

Drainage holes: The number and height of the drainage holes you poke will affect the environment in any soil-filled chamber. Sandy soil with holes poked low in the base of the chamber will mean quick drainage and drier conditions. Peaty soil and a few high drainage holes will make for wetter conditions. Create a variety of plant habitats by using different soils and drainage.

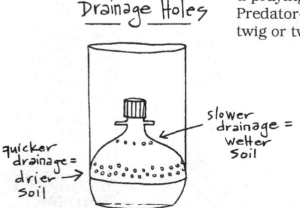

Drainage Holes

slower drainage = wetter soil

quicker drainage = drier soil

 **OBSERVE**

In your own words: Keep a careful notebook as you plan your Ecocolumn, and record exactly what you put inside. Once you have set up a column keep careful watch on how conditions change. Describe changes in your notebook. The Film Can Hand Lens (p. 109) comes in handy for examining the action in your Ecocolumn.

The tapered bottoms of the Ecocolumn chambers lend themselves to **root and soil observation**, from outside and from below. Investigate patterns of roots in different plants, and in conditions of crowding and over-watering. Also, look for worms, ants and other "critters" that inhabit the soil.

How do different types of **soils** affect your plant habitats? What happens if you change the amount of **light** a column receives? What happens if you change how **water** flows in your column? When you water the Ecocolumn with a fertilizer solution or other substance, how does it affect the column?

Do a **bioassay** (p. 93) to determine the effects of different substances on seed germination and plant development.

Explore the concept of **competition** in your column. If you place two kinds of grass in an Ecocolumn unit, does one species do better than the other? How would you measure this? Can you begin to explain what factors might make one species more successful?

Don't limit your materials to 2-liter bottles. Create ecosystems out of whatever containers you can find.

No mistakes: Remember, there is no right or wrong way to build an Ecocolumn. Change is a natural part of this experience, so when things change, try to figure out what happened and why. If insects or plants die in your Ecocolumn, think again about the natural habitat of the living creature and what it might need to live.

A few words of caution: Ecocolumns become top-heavy and tip easily. Some people Velcro them to a wall. You can also weight the bottom with gravel or water. **Avoid exposing Ecocolumns to full sunlight.**

Discussion and Essay Topics

• Consider an ecosystem such as a tropical rain forest, a prairie, or a desert. List a number of habitats you might find in these ecosystems. What types of habitats can you represent in your Ecocolumn?

• Have a discussion about **energy and nutrient cycling**. How might you explore these concepts in an Ecocolumn? Think about the energy transfer between decaying plant matter, fruit flies and predatory insects, for example. Can you illustrate this energy transfer by drawing a **food web** for your Ecocolumn?

• How does water move in your Ecocolumn, and what parts of the **water cycle** might be represented? You can model **precipitation** and **collection**, for example, and also observe **evaporation** and **condensation**. Plants in your system will allow you to discuss **transpiration**, and if you have inserted a soil column component, you'll be able to see **percolation** as water moves down through the soil.

• Explore the idea of a **closed system**, in which nothing moves in or out. If you place a cap on top of your Ecocolumn and don't poke any drainage holes in the very bottom, have you created a closed system? (Not completely, of course, since air and water vapor will circulate through the air holes, and light enters through the bottles.)

the **Nitrogen cycle**

N₂
Fixation by lightning
Atmospheric N₂
Producers
N₂ Fixation by bacteria in roots
legume
Adsorption by Producers
Consumers
Organic waste and decay
Nitrates in soil
bacteria
Decomposers

Compare this closed system to our situation on Earth. Within its surrounding atmosphere, Earth is a largely closed system. That is, water, minerals and elements such as carbon and nitrogen move in great **cycles**, constantly exchanging between air, earth, water, plants and animals. But some things do not cycle. Think about human-made, non-biodegradable items. What happens to items such as plastic? Why is it important to recycle?

In what way is Earth (and your Ecocolumn) not a closed system?

Niche Kit: *What makes a home?*

What is a niche? Is an ant's niche simply its nest? Or is the niche all the plants and animals with which an ant interacts, along with the soil it walks over and the air it breathes?

Niche, one of biology's more elusive terms, refers to all aspects of an organism's role in a community. The niche of a flowering plant, for example, includes its physical setting (soil, atmosphere, water uptake) along with other living beings that pollinate the plant, disperse its seeds, live on the surface of its roots and even eat it!

The Niche Kit will introduce you to the concept of niche and allow you to explore the complexity and interconnectedness of the ecosystems around you.

For this group activity you will need to collect samples of hypothetical niches from an area near your home or school. Small groups of students will then examine the samples to determine what sort of niche the samples might represent. Groups can also discuss what sorts of insect, animal and plant life might exist in, or interact with, this niche.

BUILD

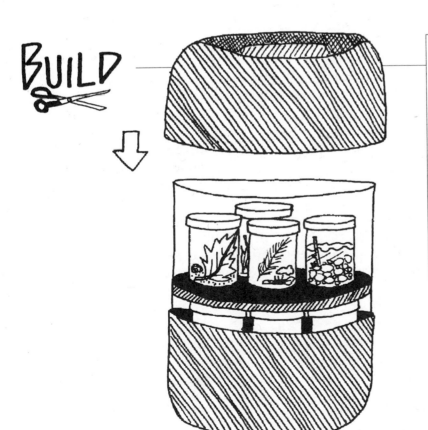

MATERIALS:

- one 2-liter bottle
- one bottle base or large plastic lid for a top
- four to eight clear film cans with caps
- round lid or cardboard cut to fit inside bottle for a divider

1. Remove label from the 2-liter bottle.

2. Cut bottle 2 to 4 cm below shoulder. Place one or two layers of clear film cans inside the bottle.

FILL

Collecting a "niche": From an area near your home or school collect samples from four to eight niches, depending on how many groups you'll be working with. Ideal sampling spots include the edges of streams and ponds, open fields, and other places with a diversity of inhabitants. Place two or three different samples from a given niche in *one* film can.

For example, in a film can representing a niche at a pond's edge you might place a few drops of water, pebbles from the shore, and a duck's feather found floating in the water. From the base of a nearby tree you could collect a piece of bark, a bit of moss from the tree's base and leaf litter. At the edge of a nearby road you might find a bit of dandelion "fluff," a piece of asphalt, and a dead moth, perhaps hit by a passing car.

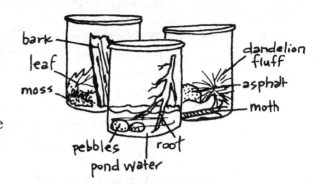

XPLORE

Know your niche: Step 1. Divide into cooperative groups of two, three or four. Each group works with one film can. The watchglass (p. 118) and the film can hand lens (p. 109) are both useful here.

Step 2. Each group describes the physical, chemical and biological characteristics of their "film can niche." Group members also list what plants, insects or animals might inhabit or interact with the niche, and then give it a name. (For example, a duck feather, a bit of car tire and a little water from a puddle might be called "roadside puddle," or if you want to get silly, "rubber ducky.")

"*Ecosculpture*"

Teacher's note: To facilitate the niche exploration, circle among the groups making observations. You may need to help students move beyond the idea of "water," for example, to "raindrop," "puddle" or "pond."

Step 3. One representative from each group then describes the group's niche to the rest of the class, summarizing pertinent details on the board, including the name of the niche.

Step 4. Finally, with everyone's help, other representatives from each group assemble to create a 3-D "ecosculpture," positioning themselves in relation to each other to represent the place of their niche in a whole system.

EXTENSION

Tropical Forest Ecocolumn: What is tropical?

What comes to mind when you hear "tropical forest?": Perhaps you think of towering trees, lush greenery, the shrieks and chatters of parrots and monkeys and perhaps even a loin-clothed individual hurtling through dappled light on the end of a hanging vine.

Tropical forests include all forests growing in the "equatorial belt" between the Tropic of Cancer and the Tropic of Capricorn. While these forests are generally very warm, they vary tremendously depending on their geography, including topography, elevation, proximity to coasts and soil type. In this exploration we will investigate some of the enormous diversity between different types of tropical forests as well as within one type of tropical rain forest.

Diversity among tropical forests: Perhaps the most familiar type of tropical forest is the **rain forest**, which typically receives at least 1250 mm (49 in.) of rain a year (some receive as much as 8000 mm, or 312 in., a year). The average temperature is 27 degrees C (81 degrees F). However, the tremendous lushness and variety of species in these rain forests are largely due to the fact that temperature and rainfall are constant throughout the year. Because there are no dramatic seasonal changes, plants thrive all year round.

Other types of tropical forests are drier and more seasonal. Some forests experience marked dry seasons in which trees shed their leaves. Three progressively drier and more seasonal types of forests are the **humid seasonal forests, savanna forests**, and **semi-arid thorn forests**. The rain forests and humid seasonal forests are often referred to together as the **tropical moist forests.**

Tropic of Capricorn

Savanna and semi-arid thorn forests experience much more variation in temperatures between day and night, receive less rainfall and may have as much as 10 drought months each year. These harsh environments support far fewer plants and animals than moist tropical forests and have a fraction of the species diversity.

There are many different types of forests within the broad categories defined above. For example, the category "tropical rain forest" includes lowland evergreen forests, semi-evergreen forests, montane or high altitude forests, heath forests, peat forests, cloud forests and swamp forests — and they are all tropical!

Diversity within a lowland rain forest: Lowland rain forests, the richest tropical forests in terms of species diversity, contain up to four general layers of vegetation. Tall, buttressed trees tower upwards, interlocking their crowns in a dense **canopy** 30 meters above. These giants absorb much of the intense tropical sunlight, allowing as little as one percent of the light to filter down to the forest floor. They also buffer the forest floor from all but the strongest winds. These trees tend to have oval-shaped leaves with an elongated "drip tip" that sheds water easily.

Sun seekers — Other plants just below the canopy take advantage of the trees and their access to sunlight. Vines climb their way up tree trunks from the dark forest floor, then sprawl out along tree branches once they near the canopy.

Another group of plants, called **epiphytes** (literally "upon plants") also inhabit the upper tree trunks and branches. These plants, including ferns, mosses, lichens, orchids, bromeliads and even cacti do not actually live off the tree like parasites, but use it for mechanical support and access to sun and nutrient-rich rainwater.

Epiphytes disperse their seeds by wind and often grow on top of one another: a fern on a moss on a lichen on a tree trunk. Because they are not in contact with the ground, these "hangers-on" must conserve their own supplies of water and nutrients. Some orchids store water in bulbous stems. Tank bromeliads have large, water-tight pockets, which can hold over two liters of water. Canopy trees have smooth or flaky bark to make it more difficult for sunlight-hungry vines and epiphytes to gain a footing.

Three Types of Tropical Forest

Forest type:	lowland rain forest	humid seasonal forest	semi-arid thorn woodland
Annual rainfall:	2000 mm (80 in)	2000 cm (80 in)	1000 mm (40 in)
Monthly rainfall:	165 mm/mo. x 12	225 mm/mo. x 8	96 mm/mo. x 10
		50 mm/mo. x 4	20 mm/mo. x 2
Annual avg. temperature:	28˚C (82˚F)	25˚C (77˚F)	28˚C (82˚F)
Annual temp. variation:	3˚C (37˚F)	18˚C (64˚F)	35˚C (95˚F)
Daily temp. variation:	8˚C (46˚F)	18˚C (64˚F)	30˚C (86˚F)

In the shade — Far below the canopy the forest **understory** is shady, humid and calm. Shade-adapted herbs, shrubs and small trees grow to several meters in height. These plants germinate and grow to maturity in the absence of any direct sunlight, although they may include species adapted to take advantage of any gaps in the canopy. If a branch or tree falls, perhaps pulled down by a heavy load of epiphytes, the gap can create a sudden column of light, photosynthetic energy for any plant that can grow quickly to take advantage of the light before the canopy closes in again.

On the forest floor — Mosses, ferns, seedlings and a layer of leaf litter lie on the forest floor. Below this fallen plant material lie tangled rootlets of forest trees and the pale mycelial strands of fungi, which rapidly decompose plant matter and recycle nutrients back into the forest.

House Plant	Origin
Cape primrose (*streptocarpus*)	South Afr. rainforest
Moss fern or spike moss (*Selaginella*)	Asian, Afr., Am. & Aust. rain forest
Miniature gloxinia (*Sinningia pusilla*)	Brazilian rain forest
Strawberry begonia (geranium) (*Saxifraga sarmentosa*)	China & Japan
Miniature African violets (*Saintpaulia*)	East Africa
Swedish ivy (*Plectranthus nummularius*)	Australia, Pacific Islands
Artillery plant (*Pilea microphylla*)	West Indies
Aluminum plant (*Pilea cadierei*)	Vietnam
Baby's tears (*Pilea depressa*)	Puerto Rico
Wandering Jew (*Tradescantia fluminensis*)	Argentina, Brazil
Spider plant (*Chlorophytum comosum*)	Cape of Good Hope
Maidenhair fern (*Adiantum*)	South American rain forest

For drier environments:

Jade plants (*Crassula argenta*),	S. Africa (Cape Province, Natal)
Mother of millions (*Kalanchoe*)	Madagascar

Plants that generally grow well in bottle environments include small-leaved ferns, small bromeliads, small-leaved ivies, mosses, liverworts, small sedum plants and small cacti.

Diversity of tropical plants: Now that you have thought about diversity between and within tropical forests, think about how plants adapt to a particular tropical climate or rain forest layer.

Many house plants are tropical plants. Gather clippings of several house plants (they can be transported wrapped in a moist paper towel). Do some research on the plants to find out their place of origin and what environments they prefer. Discuss plant and leaf size and shape, tolerance to wind, light requirements and when plants flower and bear fruit. Relate this information to what type of forest and forest layer might naturally host these plants.

Create a tropical Ecocolumn: Using your house plants, and working individually or in groups, plan and create a tropical Ecocolumn. Each Ecocolumn chamber can model a different rain forest layer. You can also model different types of tropical forest. You may have to simulate plants for some layers, providing sticks or other structural support for epiphytes, for example.

Based on the annual **rainfall**, how much water should be added to your column each day? Poke ventilation holes to decrease humidity. How much **light** are your plants receiving? What is the **temperature** in your column? A column near a light or in the sun will get very hot. How much should the temperature change during a 24-hour period? Don't forget the soil and decomposition layer.

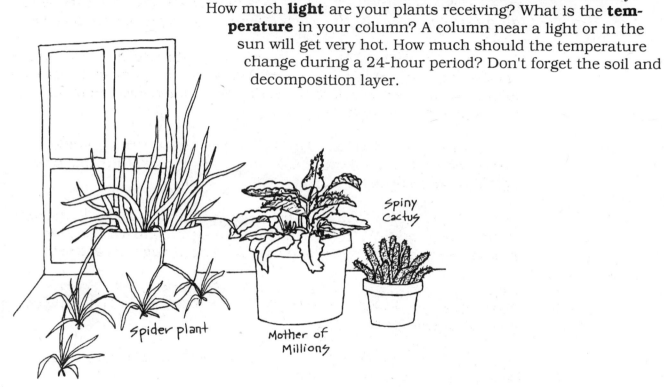

Spiny Cactus

spider plant

Mother of Millions

Rain Forest References

Forsyth, Adrian & Ken Miyata 1984. *Tropical Nature: Life and Death in the Rain Forests of Central and South America.* New York: Charles Scribner's Sons.

Meyers, Norman 1984. *The Primary Source: Tropical Forests and our Future.* New York: Norton.

Rainforests — A Teacher's Resource Guide. Compiled by Lynne Chase and available from: Rainforest Action Network, 301 Broadway, Suite A, San Francisco, CA 94133; (415) 398-4044.

Whitmore, T.C. 1990. *An Introduction to Tropical Rain Forests.* Oxford: Claredon Press.

Additional
Reading

Behnke, Frances 1972. *The Changing World of Living Things.* New York: Holt, Rinehart & Winston. *This middle school-level book introduces readers to ecological concepts such as cycles, balances and habitats.*

Corner, Thomas 1992. "Ecology in a Jar." *The Science Teacher* 59 (3): 32-37. *Middle school-level activities for introducing ecological concepts.*

Cruzan, John 1988. "Teaching Ecology with Microcosms." *The American Biology Teacher* 50(4): 226-228. *Upper-level experimental ecology labs on such topics as soil community, species interaction, nutrient cycles and biogeography.*

Culp, Mary 1990. "An Easy Method to Demonstrate Transpiration". *The American Biology Teacher*, 50 (1): 46-47. *Demonstrate this part of the water-cycle with a sunflower.*

Downer, Ann 1993. *Spring Pool: A Guide to the Ecology of Temporary Ponds.* New York: Watts. *An invitation to explore the wildlife that breeds, feeds and rests in seasonal wetlands; middle school-level.*

Hershey, David 1992. "Plants Can't Do Without CO_2." *The Science Teacher* 59 (3): 41-43. *Demonstrate the importance of this greenhouse gas using hydroponics.*

Hershey, David 1990. Accurately Measuring Transpiration." *The American Biology Teacher* 52(2): 106.

McCombs, Laurence and Rosa Nichola 1986. *What's Ecology?* New York: Addison Wesley. *A good high school-level introduction to ecology.*

Norsgaard, E. Jaediker 1990. *Nature's Great Balancing Act In Our Own Backyard.* New York: Cobblehill Books, Dutton. *An elementary to middle school-level book mostly on backyard insects.*

Spurgeon, Richard 1988. *Usborne Science & Experiments: Ecology.* London: Usborne Publishing. *A middle school-level, fun-filled book of activities and examples to illustrate the basic terms and ideas of ecology.*

Chapter 8

Big science in a small space

SCIENCE IN A FILM CAN

What makes a seed sprout? How does it know which way is up? Can a seedling discern different colors of light?

Simple in appearance, seeds have evolved over millions of years to safely transport genetic information from one generation of plants to the next. These beautifully adapted packages of botanical hope carry their own food, wear armor against flood, drought and frost, and know to wait patiently for proper germinating conditions.

You can investigate your own questions about seeds using 35 mm film cans. Seeds accomplish a great deal in a very small space, so film cans are perfect tools for seed exploration.

Film cans are also useful for growing plants, collecting insects and storing other small, important items. They are portable, so you can carry your experiments with you for round-the-clock observations.

The following experiments allow you to explore seed germination and the initial stages of plant growth and development. You can observe the effects of gravity, temperature, light and water on seedlings and seed germination. We have also included a bioassay, which allows you to test the effects of various substances on seed germination.

These experiments work best with fast-germinating seeds such as turnips, Chinese cabbage, marigolds and Wisconsin Fast Plants. For more information on any of the experiments in this chapter, write to the Wisconsin Fast Plants program (see p. 8).

GRAVITROPISM EXPERIMENTS

CONNECTIONS: *plant physiology, seed germination, gravity (gravitropism), light (phototropism), bioassay, toxicity. Scientific process skills — asking questions, observation, data recording and analysis, predicting, inferring.*

FILM CAN GERMINATION
What makes a seed sprout?

- one black 35mm film can, with lid
- three to nine seeds of a small, fast-germinating plant, such as turnips, Chinese cabbage, or Wisconsin Fast Plants (p. 8)
- water
- paper towel cut into strips 1 cm x 4 cm for wicks
- tweezers, toothpick, etc., to transport seeds

1. Add just enough water to cover bottom of film can.

2. Insert 1 to 4 wicks, tipping can to wet the strips so they adhere to sides.

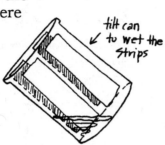

tilt can to wet the strips

3. Place 1 to 3 seeds on each wick strip.

Transport seeds on the moistened tips of tweezers (p. 117) or toothpicks.

moisten the tweezer tips

4. Place lid on can. Label can with name, date and time. Look closely at your seedlings after 24 hours, and then every day for up to a week.

DARLA
10/23/92
2:00 PM

What happens? Is germination affected if you change the amount of moisture? Do seeds germinate faster in light or in the dark? Does temperature affect germination? What kind of seeds germinate fastest?

FILM CAN GRAVITROPISM
Does a plant know which way is up?

Tropism is a plant's movement in response to a certain stimulus. Gravitropism, therefore, is the growth of a plant in response to the force of gravity.

MATERIALS:

- one black 35mm film can with cap
- one to three seedlings about 1 to 2 cm tall of a small, fast-germinating plant, such as turnips, Chinese cabbage, or Wisconsin Fast Plants (p. 8)
- water
- paper towel wick strip 1 cm x 4 cm
- scissors to cut seedling

1. Add just enough water to cover the bottom of a film can.

2. Insert wick, tipping can to moisten paper so it adheres to side of can.

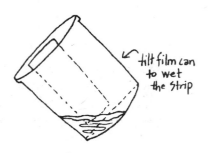

tilt film can to wet the strip

3. Cut seedlings at soil level.

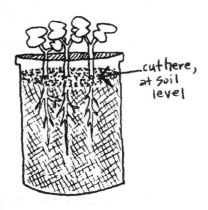

cut here, at soil level

4. Place seedlings upside-down on wet wick. Cotyledons (the seedling's first leaves) will stick to the wet wick strip. (It may be necessary to partially pull out wick while placing the seedlings.) Do NOT use tweezers to hold young plants, which are easily damaged.

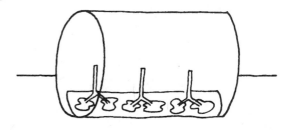

5. Cap the film can and wait 4 to 24 hours. Keep watching for up to 5 days.

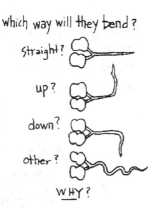

Can you predict what will happen? Make a drawing. Can you support your prediction? Carry your film can around with you to keep track of changes. How might other factors such as temperature or light affect a seedling?

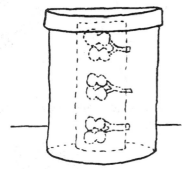

which way will they bend?

straight?

up?

down?

other?

WHY?

FILM CAN PHOTOTROPISM
Do plants prefer colors?

Tropism is a plant's movement in response to a certain stimulus. Phototropism, therefore, is the growth of a plant in response to light.

MATERIALS:

- one black 35mm film can with lid
- six seeds of a small, fast-germinating plant, such as turnips, Chinese cabbage or Wisconsin Fast Plants (p. 8)
- hole punch or awl
- clear cellophane tape
- colored transparent plastic squares (red, green, and blue), cut into squares 2 cm². Colored filters used in theater lighting work well.
- three 1 cm x 4 cm paper towel wicks

1. Punch 3 evenly spaced holes around the upper wall of a film can. A paper punch works well.

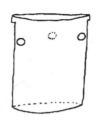

2. Tape squares of colored plastic over the holes using clear tape.

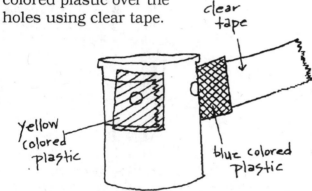

3. Add just enough water in film can to cover bottom. Slip 3 wicks onto walls of can, evenly spaced between holes. Tip can to wet wicks. Place 2 seeds each onto wicks just below the holes.

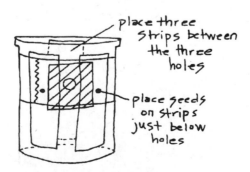

place three strips between the three holes

place seeds on strips just below holes

4. Snap lid onto can. Place under bright (not hot) light so all 3 windows receive uniform light. Look closely at your seedlings after 24 hours and then every day over the next week.

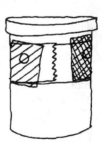

Toward which window do seedlings bend? Experiment with color. Make other chambers with three green windows opposite one blue window, or two red windows opposite one blue window. Does it matter where on the wick you place the seeds?

FILM CAN BIOASSAY
How much is too much?

A bioassay determines the impact of a certain substance on living organisms. You can use a bioassay to examine substances, such as "compost tea" from a Decomposition Column, to determine if they influence plant growth.

You can also test household substances such as sugar and coffee. At what concentration are your seeds most affected?

1. Label 4 film cans **1.0**, **0.1**, **0.01**, and **CONTROL**.

2. Add 10 drops plain water to can labeled **CONTROL**. Add 10 drops of the test solution to film can labeled **1.0**.

4. Insert one wick strip and two seeds into each can as described in germination chamber. Cover with cap.

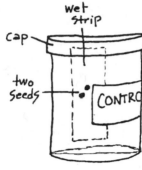

cap — wet strip

two seeds — CONTRO

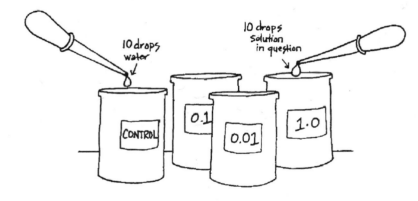

10 drops water

10 drops solution in question

CONTROL   0.1   0.01   1.0

Observe germination over the next 12 hours to 5 days. Graph how the varying concentrations of your test substance affect a specific response, such as germination rate. What other organisms can you use for a bioassay? What other substances can you test?

3. Add 9 drops of water EACH to film cans labeled **0.1**, and **0.01**. Add one drop of full strength substance from **1.0** film can to can labeled **0.1**. Mix. Take one drop of **0.1** strength solution and add to can labeled **0.01**. Mix well after each addition.

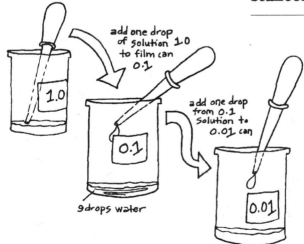

add one drop of solution 1.0 to film can 0.1

1.0

add one drop from 0.1 solution to 0.01 can

0.1

9 drops water

0.01

Additional
Reading

Clifford, Paul and Edwin Oxlade 1991. "Using Dandelion Flower Stalks for Gravitropic Studies." *The American Biology Teacher* 53(5): 290-293.

Cohen, Joy and Eve Pranis 1990. *Grow Lab Activities for Growing Minds.* Burlington, VT: National Gardening Association. *Hands-on science activities that use plants to bring science and students to life.*

De Vito, Alfred. 1991. *Recycling 35 mm Canisters for the Teaching of Science.* West Lafayette, IN: Creative Ventures, Inc. *Over 30 imaginative ways for students at all levels to investigate physics, chemistry and biology in film cans.*

Raven, Peter H. and Ray F. Evert 1981 *Biology of Plants.* New York: Worth Publishers. *Upper-level textbook, but accessibly written and well illustrated.*

Wilkins, Malcolm 1988. *Plant Watching: How Plants Remember, Tell Time, Form Relationships, and More.* New York: Facts on File.

Williams, Paul 1990. "Rapid Cycling Brassicas - a Context for Plant Biotechnology." *Biotechnology Education* 1(3): 111-114.

NOTES

Chapter 9

How does a garden grow?
GARDENING SYSTEMS

Gardens can do a lot more than just green up your school or home. You can study them, eat from them, and carry them around with you. A classroom garden will provide you with a year-round supply of study subjects with which to explore the relationships between plants and environmental factors such as soil, light and water.

You can also grow food plants such as basil, lettuce, oregano and parsley, and have a salad feast.

These gardening systems are portable, so you can take them home during vacations.

You can also create miniature plant worlds in bottle caps with mosses and liverworts and carry them around with you for observation. All of these designs have built-in watering systems for the plants — perfect for the lazy gardener or the busy teacher.

The gardening systems shown in this chapter are just a few of many ways you can put throw-away materials to good use growing plants (see the Terrarium, p. 110). Use your imagination and the contents of your trash can to come up with other ideas.

Bottle Cap Garden

 **CONNECTIONS:** *gardening, plant growth and development, plant physiology, life cycles, capillary action, engineering and design. Scientific process skills — organization, classification, data observation and recording.*

The soil: How a plant grows depends in part on the water and nutrients provided by the soil. With our gardening systems we have used soil made with equal amounts of peat and vermiculite. You can also use commercial potting soils or experiment with creating your own soils (see Soil Meditations p. 33).

The water: Our gardening systems use wicks: strips of material that bring a constant source of water from a reservoir to plant roots. Wicking works by **capillary action**, the phenomenon responsible for the way water moves along the fibers of paper towels and cotton string. You have probably noticed that if you wet one end of a paper towel, the water spreads rapidly toward the rest of the material, even against the force of gravity. How does this work?

Water molecules are attracted to any hydrophilic, or water-friendly, surface such as paper, cotton and glass. In a towel, for example, water molecules are attracted to the cotton fibers and water spreads from one corner toward the rest of the towel. The water molecules in contact with the fibers pull along other water molecules, and the towel becomes saturated with water.

Capillarity is also responsible for the way water molecules in a glass tube creep upwards along the inside. The water molecules in contact with the tube also pull along other water molecules, and the water level rises in a slight "U" shape. (When determining the amount of water in a glass graduated cylinder, therefore, you should always measure from the center of the water level.)

Capillarity does not occur in a plastic tube because plastic has no charge to attract water molecules.

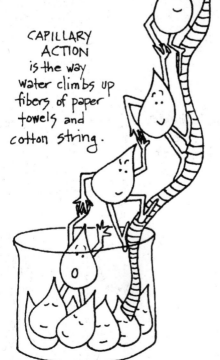

CAPILLARY ACTION is the way water climbs up fibers of paper towels and cotton string.

The wick: Our favorite wicking material is **fabric interfacing**, a felt-like synthetic available at fabric stores. It must be washed thoroughly with detergent before using in order to remove a flame retardant toxic to plants. After washing, rinse the interfacing well, and hang it to dry. Soak the material again before using it in order to start capillary action.

Cotton string and disposable kitchen wipes make good short-term wicks. Because of microbial activity in the soil these wicks will disintegrate within a couple of months. Experiment with different brands of utility wipes and synthetic string, but make sure all materials wick successfully before you depend on them.

Saturate all wicks with water before inserting them into growing systems. This ensures that water is moving through the wick and is not obstructed by air bubbles. Wicks should run from the bottom of the reservoir up into the soil, but not protrude above the soil surface or end up stuck against the side of the growing system.

*Soak all wicking material **before** adding soil to the system in order to start capillary action.*

The light: You can successfully grow plants using cool white fluorescent tubes, which are the same lights used in schools. Sunlight is a blend of all the colors in the spectrum. Cool white fluorescent tubes emit more light on the blue end of the spectrum, warm fluorescent bulbs have more light rays in the red end of the spectrum and incandescent bulbs emit even more red light. "Grow" lights sold in stores emit light across more of the full spectrum, but are not necessary.

Setting up an inexpensive light system is simple and very rewarding, especially if you don't have access to sunny windowsills. Keep the lights three to six inches from the tops of the plants to ensure the best plant growth. You can do this by placing the plants on empty containers to raise them toward the light (see the Grow Bucket p. 105), or lowering the light toward the plants as in the adjustable system shown here. (For a list of **plants suited for small growing systems**, see the Terrarium, p. 110.)

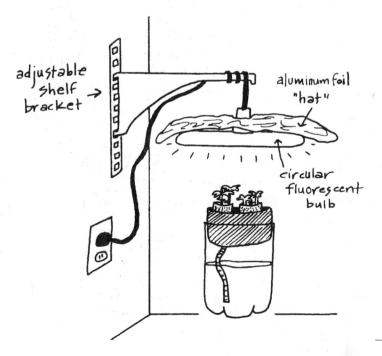

adjustable shelf bracket →

aluminum foil "hat"

circular fluorescent bulb

Adjustable growing system: Suspend a socket and light bulb from a shelf bracket, ringstand, or other suitable hanger. We use 30-watt circular cool fluorescent white bulbs. This system adjusts easily to the height of plants. Make a reflective "hat" for the bulb out of aluminum foil or an aluminum pie plate so more light reflects toward the plants.

FILM CAN WICKPOTS

MATERIALS:

- 35 mm film cans
- 3 cm-long pieces of cotton string or strips of fabric interfacing
- nail poke (p. 6)
- seeds, soil, distilled water

Plastic 35 mm film cans make wonderful pots for small plants like mosses, ferns, oregano, babies' tears, miniature African violets and Wisconsin Fast Plants (see p. 8), and for sprouting larger plants.

The pots are made to be used in conjunction with a wicking system like the Bottle Base Reservoir (see p. 101). You can obtain film cans free from any film developing outlet.

3. Fill the cans with soil. Add seeds or plants. Water. Mosses and ferns prefer distilled water.

NOTE: Do not press soil

1. Poke or drill a 0.5 cm hole in bottom of 35 mm film can.

nail poke

2. Insert a 3 cm piece of premoistened cotton string.

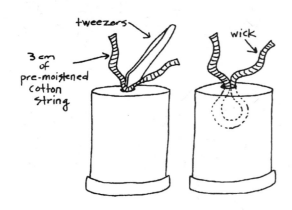

tweezers

3 cm of pre-moistened cotton string

wick

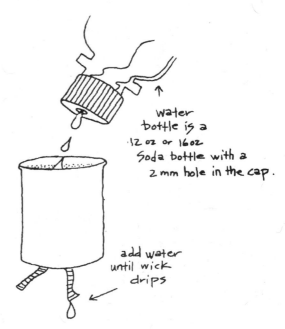

water bottle is a 12 oz or 16oz soda bottle with a 2 mm hole in the cap.

add water until wick drips

BOTTLE BASE RESERVOIR

A Bottle Base Reservoir will provide enough water to keep your film can wickpots watered for a month!

MATERIALS:

- one 1- or 2-liter soda bottle (green bottles reduce algal growth)
- one base from another same-sized soda bottle or a plastic container such as cottage or cream cheese dish with a 1-2 cm hole for wick poked near bottom edge
- plastic lid or petri dish to fit inside base or dish to make a flat platform
- wick strip 1 cm x 25 cm (p. 98)
- wick pad large enough to cover the plastic lid (p. 98)
- Bottle Biology Tool Kit (p. 2)

1. Remove bottle label and cut off the top. Where you cut the bottle depends on how tall a reservoir you want to make. Shorter reservoirs work better in Grow Buckets.

2. Enlarge or create a 1 to 2 cm hole in a bottle base or plastic dish to accommodate the wick. Make two or three 2 cm-long slits in reservoir to accommodate base or dish.

Set the base or plastic container into the reservoir. Insert the plastic lid or petri dish to act as a platform.

Saturate the wick strip and wick pad thoroughly. Thread wick strip through the hole in the plastic container or base so it runs from the *bottom* of the reservoir and across platform. Lay wick pad on top of the platform over the wet strip.

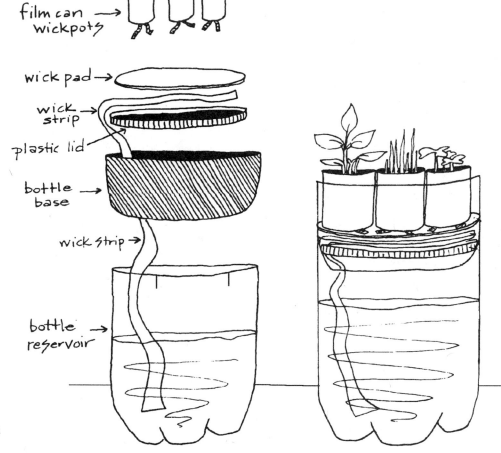

film can wickpots

wick pad

wick strip

plastic lid

bottle base

wick strip

bottle reservoir

3. Place film can wickpots with wet wicks firmly on top of wick pad. Make sure there is good contact between the wicks and wick pad.

TerrAqua Bottle

MATERIALS:

• one 1- or 2-liter bottle
• one bottle cap
• wick strip 25 cm x 1 cm
• Bottle Biology Tool Kit
  (p. 2)

A TerrAqua Bottle will allow you to grow larger plants. This is a single bottle version of the TerrAqua Column (see p. 62).

1. Remove label and cut 1 cm below shoulder.

cut 1cm below shoulder

2. Poke or drill a 1 cm hole in bottle cap.

1 cm hole in cap

3. Thread a thoroughly wet wick strip through bottle top, invert top, and set into base. Wick should reach bottom of reservoir and thread loosely through cap.

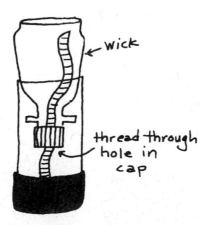

← wick

thread through hole in cap

4. Fill reservoir with water. Add soil and plants to top chamber. To be effective, the wick should run up into soil, not be plastered along a side of the bottle.

For better drainage place a layer of gravel, sand, or vermiculite in the bottom of the soil unit.

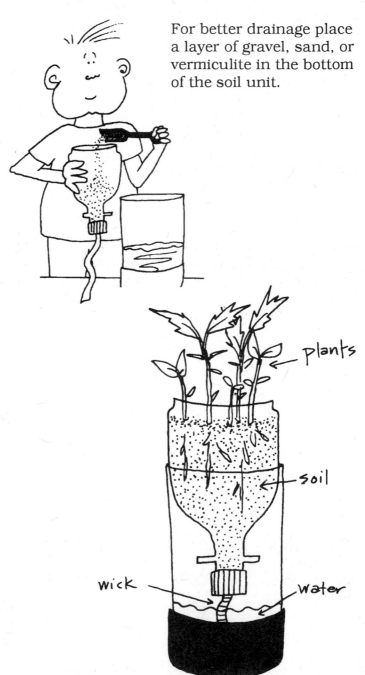

← plants

← soil

wick →

→ water

Bottle Cap Gardens

Create a growing system for some of the world's tinier plants.

Materials:

- one 1-liter soda bottle
- plastic lid to fit inside base
- wicking pad cut to match diameter of plastic lid (p. 98)
- three to five bottle caps
- three to five 3-cm long pieces of cotton string
- Bottle Biology Tool Kit (p. 2)
- small plants: small ferns, liverworts, mosses (see p. 110 for other plants)
- distilled water

1. Remove label and base from bottle. Cut bottle 2 cm below shoulder.

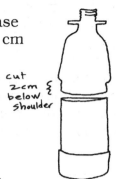

cut 2cm below shoulder

2. Cut 3 or 4 1 cm-long slits around top.

cut 3 or 4 1cm-long slits in top

5. Fill caps with soil, and water gently until string drips. Use distilled water only for ferns, mosses and liverworts.

water gently until wick drips

Fill with soil

3. Use an awl or drill to poke holes in bottle caps. Enlarge with a tapered reamer to about 0.5 cm in diameter.

poke hole in cap with awl...

...then enlarge with tapered reamer.

6. Place small plants or cuttings into caps. Tape over any holes in base and place plastic lid inside bottle base for a platform. Place a saturated wick pad on top of platform. Put caps onto platform. Cover. You can attach a bottle cap as well to prevent the terrarium from drying out, but poke a few air holes in the bottle top.

4. Insert a saturated loop of cotton string.

wick pad →

platform →

base →

FILM CAN GARDEN

Clear film cans make good homes for the tiny ferns and moss you plant in single bottle cap gardens. You can also replace the film can garden top with a film can hand lens (p. 109), and bring your tiny plant world into closer view.

MATERIALS:

- one clear film can with cap
- one soda bottle cap
- cotton string wick
- soil, water, mosses, ferns, liverworts and other small plants
- Bottle Biology Tool Kit (p. 2)
- distilled water

1. Cut a clear film can in half with scissors.

2. Use an awl or drill to poke a hole in the center of the bottle cap. Enlarge with a tapered reamer to about 0.5 cm in diameter.

poke hole in cap with awl...

...then enlarge with tapered reamer.

3. Use a scissors to cut off protruding rim of cap so it slides inside film can.

cut off rim

4. Insert a saturated 3mm-long loop of cotton string into hole.

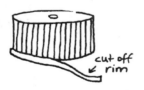

insert moist loop of cotton string

5. Fill cap with soil and water gently until string drips. Use distilled water only for mosses, ferns and liverworts.

water gently until wick drips

Fill with soil

6. Place small plants or cuttings into soil. Poke a small air hole in the bottom half of the film can and add distilled water. Fit the film can onto the bottom of the bottle cap, just halfway. This will allow you to fit the top half of film can onto the top of the cap. Poke a few air holes in the film can cap and snap in place. You can also replace the film can top with a film can hand lens to get a better look at your plants (see p. 109).

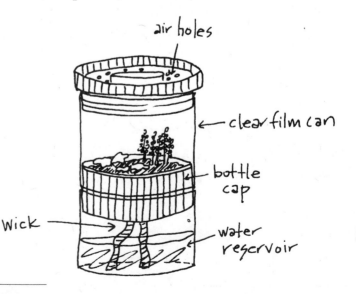

air holes

clear film can

bottle cap

wick

water reservoir

GROW BUCKET

MATERIALS:

- five gallon plastic bucket with lid
- heavy duty utility knife, key hole saw or small electric hand saw if you are cutting many buckets
- two-piece utility light bulb socket
- light weight electrical wire (lamp cord) with plug
- circular fluorescent light bulb (30-watt bulbs work well)

If your classroom lacks sunny windows, the Grow Bucket will help plants grow green and healthy anywhere.

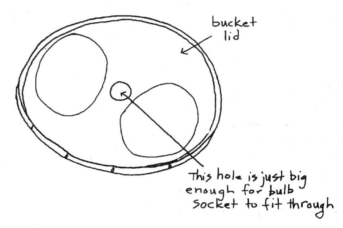

bucket lid

This hole is just big enough for bulb socket to fit through

1. Cutting ventilation holes. Cut 2 holes about 7 - 8 cm in diameter opposite each other on lower part of bucket. You can initiate a cut by drilling a hole with a hand or electric drill on your cutting line in order to insert a utility knife or keyhole saw.

Also, cut 2 holes 7.5 cm in diameter opposite each other on the lid of the bucket. Leave as much space as possible between the holes to allow room to mount the light bulb socket.

These 4 holes will encourage air circulation so that the air temperature inside the bucket is as close as possible to room temperature (18 to 24 degrees C; 65 to 75 degrees F). (Continued on the next page.)

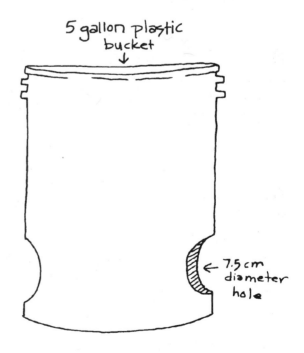

5 gallon plastic bucket

← 7.5 cm diameter hole

2. Mounting the bulb. To mount the light fixture in the lid, cut a hole in the center of the lid just big enough to accept the metal shaft of a two-piece utility light bulb socket. (If electricity is not your thing, ask assistance from someone at a hardware store or a school custodian.) Connect the electrical cord. Screw bulb into socket.

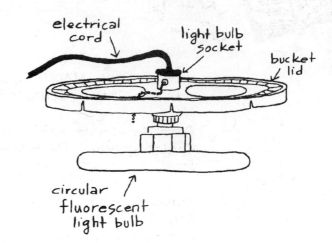

electrical cord

light bulb socket

bucket lid

circular fluorescent light bulb

3. Making a door. Although you can reach plants through the lid of the bucket, a side door cut out of the bucket makes this easier and looks good too. Our doors measure 20 cm wide by 26 cm tall and begin at the bottom of the bucket. Duct tape makes a decent hinge, or you can use small metal hinges. Duct tape or a small hook-and-eye will keep the door closed.

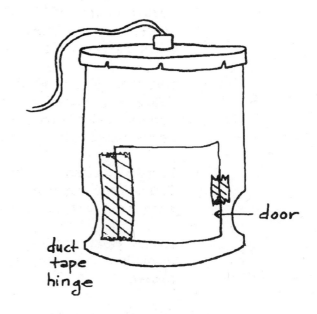

door

duct tape hinge

4. Positioning plants. Place Bottle Reservoirs and other plant containers as close to the bulb as possible so they get plenty of light. You can place plants on stacked bottle bases so that the tops of the plants are 2 to 4 cm from the bulb.

Berg, Virginia 1993. "Tips for Teaching Plant-Water Relations." *The American Biology Teacher* 55(2): 96-98. *Upper level.*

Davis, Lawrence 1993. "Negative Gravitropic Responses Induced by Centrifugation." *The American Biology Teacher* 55(2): 104-5. *Upper level.*

Kindersley, Dorling 1993. *Eyewitness Visual Dictionary of Plants.* NY: Eyewitness Books, Knopf. *A well-illustrated reference for a large number of plants and their ecosystems.*

Muller, Gerda 1993. *The Garden in the City.* New York: Dutton. *An elementary-level guide and story about how a family works together to plant a garden in their new city home.*

National Gardening Association 1988. *Grow Lab: A Complete Guide to Gardening in the Classroom.* Burlington, VT: National Gardening Association. *A hands-on science curriculum that uses plants to bring science and students to life.*

Pringle, Laurence 1983. *Being A Plant.* New York: Thomas Y. Crowell. *This middle school-level book is a friendly, well-written introduction to such plant topics as water movement, pollination and seeds.*

Raven, Peter and Ray Evert 1981. *Biology of Plants.* New York: Worth Publishers. *A college-level textbook; accessibly written and well illustrated.*

Schumann, Donna 1980. *Living With Plants: A Guide to Practical Botany.* Eureka, CA: Mad River Press. *A gardener's handbook on how plants grow and how to help them grow well.*

Wilkins, Malcolm 1988. *Plant Watching: How Plants Remember, Tell Time, Form Relationships and More.* New York: Facts on File. *If you don't already think that plants are fascinating, exciting, and ready to take over the world whenever they choose, this book will convince you. (Written for an adult audience.)*

sniff
sniff

Chapter 10

BOTTLE INSTRUMENTS AND DEVICES

Living in a hi-tech, computerized world, we sometimes underestimate the potential of everyday objects as tools for investigation and exploration.

Great inventors and scientists have always relied on good observational skills and imaginative uses of ordinary items. Think about Benjamin Franklin and his kite, for example, or Isaac Newton and the apple. The following collection of tools, made primarily of soda bottles and film cans, will help you observe, measure, weigh, time and compare the results of your Bottle Biology explorations.

This chapter begins with the Film Can Hand Lens. You can use the lens to explore two other constructions in this chapter, the terrarium and the aquarium, which have initiated many people into the practice of turning trash into treasure.

FILM CAN HAND LENS

1. Drill or melt a 20 mm hole in the bottom of the bottle cap. You may find it helpful to trim the small protruding rim off the cap with scissors so it will slide into the film can.

2. Drill or melt a 20 mm hole in the bottom of the clear film can. (Drill smaller holes in the film can for smaller lenses.)

3. Slide the lens into the film can. Push the bottle cap down into the can until it holds the lens snugly in place. Poke two small holes in sides of film can for a neck string. Snap cap on the film can. (You can also drill or melt two optional holes for access ports as shown at right.)

MATERIALS:
- one clear film can
- one soda bottle cap
- one double convex lens about 28 mm in diameter and with a 59 mm focal length. The lens diameter needs to be less than that of the film can. Glass and plastic lenses are available for about $5 from lab suppliers. (p. 8).
- Bottle Biology Tool Kit (p. 2)

cut off rim

20 mm hole

20 mm hole

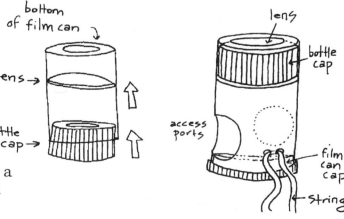

bottom of film can

lens →

bottle cap →

lens

bottle cap

access ports

film can cap

string

TERRARIUM

MATERIALS:
- one 2-liter soda bottle
- Bottle Biology Tool Kit (p. 2)
- gravel, soil and terrestrial life

1. Remove the label from your bottle and the base, if it has one.

2. Cut the bottle according to what sort of top you want on your terrarium. If your bottle does not have a removable base, you can use the footed base with a plastic lid set inside to serve as a platform.

terrarium tops

terrarium base

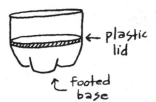

← plastic lid

↑ footed base

3. Poke air holes in top. Begin with 3-4 "x's" of holes, and add more if your terrarium appears too wet. Cut three 3 cm-long slits in top so it slides into base.

air ← holes

cut slits to make top fit into base

4. Fill the terrarium base with a layer of sand or gravel for drainage, then soil (garden, woodland, or potting soil). You might also add a little gardener's charcoal to keep the soil in good condition.

5. Add plants or seeds. Water the soil well at first, but rarely thereafter unless no moisture condenses on the inside of the terrarium top.

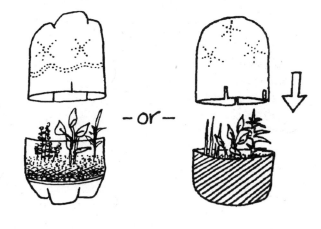

–or–

Recommended terrarium plants:
Small-leaved, slow-growing plants work best such as Strawberry begonia, small-leaved oregano or thyme, Moss fern (Selaginella), artillery plants (Pilea microphylla), babies' tears (Pilea depressa), Swedish ivy and miniature African violets. Ferns, mosses and liverworts also do well, but use only distilled water or rainwater.

For a drier, desert-like terrarium, plant leaves of jade (Crassula argenta), sedum plants and small cacti in well-drained, sandy soil.

AQUARIUM

MATERIALS:

- one 2-liter soda bottle
- one extra base from another bottle, another bottle bottom or a plastic container to act as a lid
- Bottle Biology Tool Kit (p. 2)
- water and aquatic life

1. Remove the label from your bottle.

2. Cut off the bottle top 1 to 2 cm above shoulder where bottle tapers. For an aquarium top, use the plastic base from another bottle or a plastic container. Poke air holes.

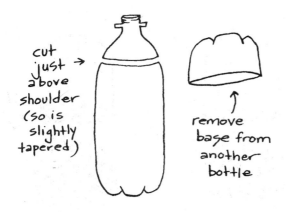

cut just above shoulder (so is slightly tapered)

remove base from another bottle

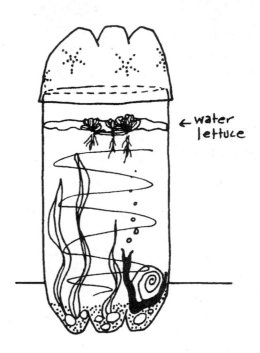

← water lettuce

3. Place sand or pond sediment on the bottom of your aquarium. Water from a pond or lake will have more microscopic organisms than tap water.

Fill your aquarium with small aquatic life, such as snails, insects, duckweed, algae, water lettuce, *Elodea* and Hornwort or Coontail (*Ceratophyllum demersum*).

Fill with water and:

snails

water plants

sand and pebbles

BOTTLE MICROSCOPE

MATERIALS:

- one 1-liter soda bottle
- propane torch
- 17 to 20 mm diameter test tube
- aluminum foil
- bamboo cooking skewer
- double stick Velcro tape
- two #3 rubber stoppers
- four 9 cm plastic petri plates
- one clear 35 mm film can
- glass microscope slide
- 22 to 29 mm diameter 5X lens
  Glass and plastic lenses can be
  purchased for about $5 from lab
  supply companies, (see p. 8)
- Bottle Biology Tool Kit (p. 2)

Note: This is a project for the committed bottle tinkerer!

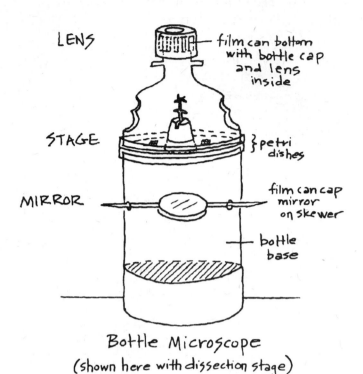

LENS — film can bottom with bottle cap and lens inside

STAGE — } petri dishes

MIRROR — film can cap mirror on skewer

bottle base

Bottle Microscope
(shown here with dissection stage)

3. Dissection stage: Make a 1-cm deep cut in stopper. Push stopper up through hole in plates. Specimens can be inserted in stopper cut.

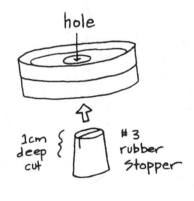

hole

1cm deep cut { #3 rubber stopper

1. Cut bottle:
Remove label from soda bottle and cut bottle 2-3 cm below shoulder.

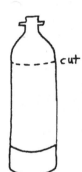

cut

2. Dissection stage:
Heat the lip of a test tube with a torch or candle, and melt a 22 mm hole through the center of two petri plates held *back to back*. The plates will fuse together.

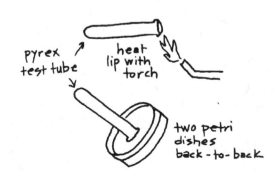

pyrex test tube → heat lip with torch

two petri dishes back-to-back

Dissection Stage

Bottle Microscope cont. ————————————

4. Transmission stage: Cut a second stopper in half lengthwise. Place a Velcro patch on the bottom of each stopper half and on either side of petri plate hole. Mount as shown. Specimens can be placed on 1/2 of a glass slide (made by scoring the slide widthwise with a diamond or Carborundum and snapping it in half) on the rubber stopper stand.

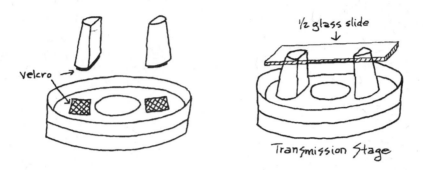

Transmission Stage

5. Mirror: Poke two holes opposite each other in the rim of film can cap. Wrap or glue shiny foil on the cap for mirror surface. Poke two opposing holes in bottle base. Thread the bamboo skewer through base and film can cap as shown.

Poke holes in film can cap

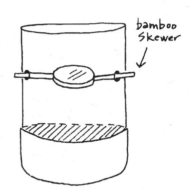

bamboo skewer

6. Lens: Melt or drill 20 mm holes in bottle cap and in film can bottom. Cut off film can 1.5 cm from bottom. For 24 to 29 mm lenses insert lens into film can and push bottle cap into can to hold lens into place. For 22 to 24 mm lenses omit film can and sandwich lens between bottle cap and bottle neck.

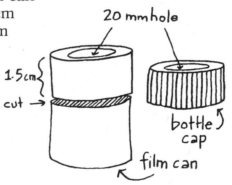

20 mm hole

1.5 cm

cut →

bottle cap

film can

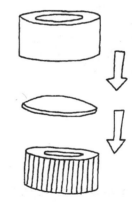

7. Melt access holes: Reheat the test tube and melt overlapping holes in bottle top to provide access to stage. Assemble the microscope according to the picture on the preceding page.

FILM CAN MICROSCOPE

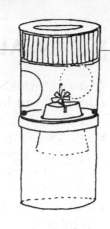

This construction is similar to the Film Can Hand Lens, except it provides you with a holder for small specimens.

MATERIALS:

- two film cans, one clear, one black
- one soda bottle cap
- one double convex lens, 28 mm in diam. We suggest a focal length of 59 mm. You can use a smaller lens by drilling a correspondingly smaller hole in the film can. Glass and plastic lenses can be purchased for about $5 from lab supply companies such as Edmund Scientific (see p. 8).
- #3 rubber stopper
- straight pins with large glass or plastic round heads
- Bottle Biology Tool Kit (see p. 2)

makes a nice necklace, too!

1. Drill or melt 20 mm (3/4 in.) holes in the bottom and sides of the clear film can and in the plastic soda bottle cap. You may find it helpful to cut off the small protruding rim of the cap with scissors. Drop lens into film can and slide in bottle cap as shown so it holds lens snugly in place.

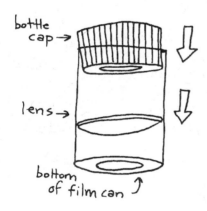

bottle cap →

lens →

bottom of film can ↑

3. Make a cut 1 cm deep into the small end of the rubber stopper. The slit will open when you squeeze the stopper so you can hold a flower, insect or other specimen to examine. Assemble microscope as shown.

2. Drill a 20 cm (3/4 in.) hole in the lid of the black film can. Insert three large, round-headed pins evenly spaced around the perimeter of the lid. The clear film can will "snap" on over the pins on the lid.

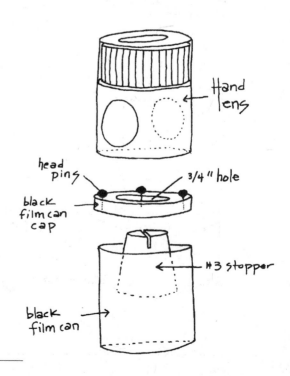

Hand lens

head pins

3/4" hole

black film can cap

#3 stopper

black film can

BOTTLE BALANCE

MATERIALS:

- two identical 2-liter bottles
- small 3 cm-long piece of dowel or round pencil
- wooden strip or molding approx. 3 cm x 0.5 cm x 42 cm (a yard stick cut in half and glued double works well)
- four 1/3 in. wood screws with washers
- Velcro strips
- Bottle Biology Tool Kit (p. 2)

1. Remove labels and bases from the two bottles. (If you have only footed bottles, cut off footed bases from other bottles to act as stands, or look for two other identical containers that can act as stands.)

2. Tape or glue dowel to exact center of wooden stick.

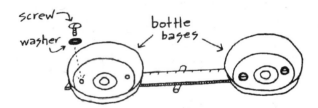

wooden dowel or pencil

tape

3. Screw bottle bases, or two other containers for stands, onto ends of wooden stick, equidistant from center. Feed screws through the pre-existing holes in the base.

screw

washer

bottle bases

4. Attach velcro strips to bottle base and bottom on each side of the balance. You may need to build up the Velcro a bit so it comes in full contact with the bottle bottom.

Alternatively, you can use a 1-liter graduated cylinder with the sides of the base removed, as shown below (see p. 117).

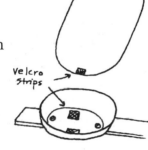

Velcro strips

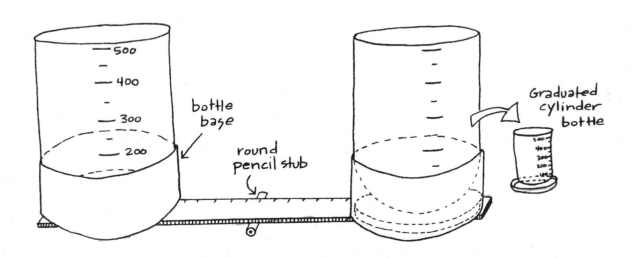

500
400
300
200

bottle base

round pencil stub

Graduated cylinder bottle

BOTTLE TIMER

MATERIALS:

- two 1-liter bottles (or smaller) with caps
- 3/4 liter of salt or clean, dry sand
- one film can
- Bottle Biology Tool Kit (p. 2)

1. Remove labels from two bottles. Fill one about 3/4 full of salt or sand.

Sand

2. Melt or poke equally sized large holes in each bottle cap. Place caps on bottles.

hole

cap

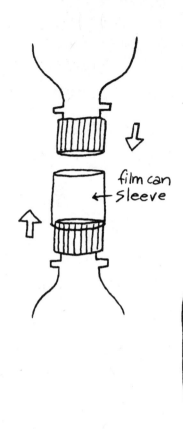

film can
sleeve

3. Slice bottom of film can off to make a sleeve. Fit capped soda bottles into either end of sleeve. Tape securely.

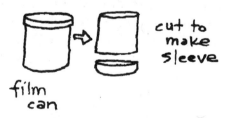

film can

cut to make sleeve

How precise is your bottle timer? Run some test trials with a watch. You can change the rate of the timer by cutting quarter-sized discs out of cardboard with different sized holes in the center and placing them between the bottle caps.

More Treasures from Trash

TWEEZERS

trim off corners

cut

tweezers

laundry detergent bottle

PEAS

PEAS

WATER BOTTLE

water bottle

hole in cap

GRADUATED FUNNEL

500
400
300
200
100

GRADUATED CYLINDER

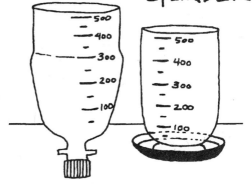

500
400
300
200
100

A 1-liter bottle has a volume of 1050 mls or ccs. To make a graduated cylinder, add water 50 mls at a time using a premeasured graduated cylinder or another measuring vessel. Mark off each 50 ml increment with a permanent marker to the 500 ml point. Then empty the bottle and cut it about 0.5 cm above the 500 ml level.

The top half of the bottle can be capped, inverted into the bottom half, and marked off by 50 mls as above. Remove the cap and use it as a graduated funnel.

Once you make one bottle you can use it as a guide to make others like it.

FILM CAN FLASHLIGHT

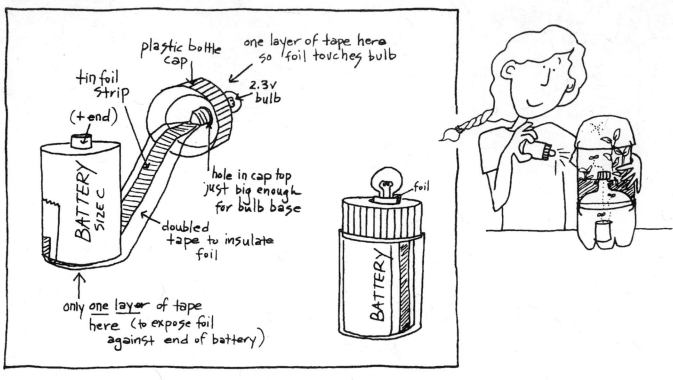

plastic bottle cap

one layer of tape here so foil touches bulb

tin foil strip

2.3v bulb

(+ end)

BATTERY SIZE C

hole in cap top just big enough for bulb base

doubled tape to insulate foil

only one layer of tape here (to expose foil against end of battery)

foil

BATTERY

TWINE DISPENSER

poke hole in cap

cut

base

BOTTLE BOTTOM WATCHGLASS

use clear bottle bottoms to make "watchglasses" for collecting and observing small things

NOTES ——————————————————————

INDEX

This index should give you easy access to the text. It is designed to point you to the major topics and ideas discussed in the book, and will allow easy use of selected activities and sections.

Index prepared by Dave Wuolu